Creative Costumes
& Halloween Décor

50 Projects to Sew & Craft

Creative Publishing
international

Creative Publishing
international

Copyright © 1997, 1998, 2008
Creative Publishing International, Inc.
400 First Avenue North
Suite 300
Minneapolis, MN 55401
1-800-328-3895
www.creativepub.com

ISBN-13: 978-1-58923-360-7
ISBN-10: 1-58923-360-3

10 9 8 7 6 5 4 3 2 1

Proofreader Julie M. Bartynski
Book Design Indicia Design, Tiffany Cooper
Cover Design 4 Eyes Design
Page Layout Indicia Design

Printed in China

Contents

Introduction 4

Creative Costumes 6

Halloween Décor 120

Patterns 228
Index 239

INTRODUCTION

Halloween occurs at the time of the year when the last of the harvest is being gathered, the days are cooler, and the nights come earlier and seem more mysterious. It's a time for children of all ages to enjoy the preparations as they invite witches and monsters and hobgoblins home.

Halloween festivities revolve around costumes. The adventure and merriment of the occasion are fueled by the creative collection of masqueraders. Original costumes always attract the most attention, much to the amusement of the wearer. It is no wonder Halloween has become one of the busiest seasons for the home sewing industry. After all, sewing and creativity go hand in hand.

In Creative Costumes (page 6) you will discover ways to design and sew distinctive costumes. By breaking the total costume down into separate elements, you can build a costume that is as simple or detailed as you wish. Similar construction techniques are used for various elements throughout the book, making them very compatible.

In Halloween Décor (page 120), there are a variety of projects that will help you greet your costumed visitors, from traditional pumpkin carving and child-friendly pumpkin painting to scarecrows and life-size figures for the front door.

Decorate your home with wreaths, swags, and tripods that showcase the season. Create a bone-clattering skeleton, a spiderweb mobile, or a small haunted house. Quilt a scarecrow wall hanging. Prop wooden shelf sitters next to whimsical picture frames or on a bewitching shelf. Dispel the gloom with lighted swags.

Celebrate the season with a party. Make intriguing invitations from ordinary paper bags. Decorate your table with runners, placemats, napkins, and coasters just right for the season. Make wired felt place cards and foam treat cups for your guests, and serve them Halloween goodies on painted glass. Set the stage with a haunting centerpiece, bathed in the eerie glow of spook-inspired candlelight.

Get creative, have some fun, and enjoy the Halloween season!

Creative
Costumes

8 Costume Styles

16 Tabards

20 Design-blocked Tabards

22 Legs, Tails, and Stingers

28 Raw-edge Appliqués

30 Gowns

36 Full Suit Costumes

40 Headwear

42 Witch Hats

46 Medieval Hats

50 Crowns and Halos

54 Padded Hoods

60 Simple Headgear

68 Capes, Skirts, and Wings

70 Capes

76 Skirts

82 Bat Wings

88 Padded Wings

92 Sheer Wings

96 Finishing Touches

98 Collars

102 Arm and Leg Accents

108 Gloves

112 Spats

116 Wands and Scepters

Costume Styles

FOUNDATION GARMENTS

Various garments are suitable to serve as the foundation of a costume. Some can be purchased inexpensively, while others can be sewn following simple instructions or by using basic patterns.

Costumes that consist of a tabard (page 16) and assorted accessories require very simple undergarments.

Depending on the climate, these may include a leotard and tights or, for more warmth, a fleece sweatshirt and pants. Measurements for the outer costume should always be taken over these undergarments.

A gown may be the basic garment needed for a variety of costumes, such as a witch, a wizard, a princess, an angel, and many others. Any basic gown pattern can be used, or a simple gown can be folded, cut, and sewn, following the instructions on page 30. The distinguishing characteristics of the gown costume are derived from the fabric selected as well as the embellishments and accessories that are added to it.

Simple costumes for toddlers and older children can be created from purchased sleepers and a few creative embellishments and accessories. Or basic sleeper, pajamas, jumpsuit, and sweat suit patterns can be modified, as on page 36, to create many costumes, from assorted animals to vegetables to wherever your imagination takes you.

COSTUME EXAMPLES

The examples shown here and on the following pages illustrate many combinations of costume elements that can be sewn, following the instructions in this book.

ZINNIA

grew from a basic leotard and tights. A padded hood with petals blooms around her face; a leaf skirt encircles her waist; and leafy gathered wristlets, anklets, and collar complete the transformation. A whimsical dragonfly is painted on her cheek.

WITCH

makes the Halloween scene in a hat, gown, and cape. Gloves with long green fingernails clutch her broom. Store-bought hair sets off her eerie, painted face.

JACK-O'-LANTERN

consists of a tabard worn over a sweat suit. The leafy gathered collar, wristlets, and anklets testify to her roots in the plant kingdom.

FAIRY PRINCESS

wears a full-overlay skirt over a leotard and tights. Sparkly padded wings, halo-style crown, and glitzy star wand feed the fantasy. Gathered collar, wristlets, and anklets give her a magical aura.

LION COSTUME

sewn from a jumpsuit pattern, boasts a terrific tail, furry tummy insert, and shoe flaps. The proud mane, attached to a padded hood, is the purr-fect frame for a cute face.

SUPERHERO

wears sleek-fitting pants and top. Padded spats, armbands, and collar are emblazoned with layered metallic appliqués. Padded headband and belt are sewn with the same techniques.

ANGEL

floats about in a gathered-sleeve gown, adorned with decorative cord. Star-spangled padded wings are worn with an elastic harness, hidden under the gown. A shimmery halo is proof of her innocence.

MAGICIAN

wears a knee-length lined cape over plain black pants and shirt. Add a curled mustache and a hat deep enough to hide a bunny, and—presto!—you have a costume.

BUMBLEBEE TABARD

sewn with stinger, sheer wings, and extra legs, can be worn over any weather-wise clothing. Perky antennae and glossy eyes transform an ordinary ball cap.

BABY BEE

buzzes around in a design-blocked hooded sleeper with detachable sheer wings and springy antennae. How sweet!

PETS' COSTUMES

require some modifications. Half-circle cape allows free movement; hats are made in miniature.

BUTTERFLY

flits into view, wearing appliquéd padded wings attached to a tabard. A restyled ball cap sports glossy eyes and metallic antennae. Inexpensive canvas shoes are painted to match the costume. Undergarments can be selected to suit the weather.

WIZARD

conjures up Halloween fun, wearing a gown and cape. Celestial accents twinkle, from his hat to his cheeks to his glow-in-the-dark wand.

DRAGON COSTUME
worn over tight-fitting undergarments, includes a design-blocked tabard with shaped, spiked tail and padded wings. The padded hood has horns, ears, glossy eyes, and spikes. Claw-tipped gloves and knee-high spats reinforce the theme, while face paint enhances a ferocious expression.

ROBOT
costume includes a tabard dotted with gadgets, vent hose leggings and armbands, and padded spats. These elements, sewn from metallic fabrics, are worn over tight-fitting clothes. Effective details include spray-painted gloves, an aluminum pail hat, and some imaginative face painting.

GYPSY
whirls in her long gathered skirt, adorned at the waist with a trinket-trimmed scarf. Purchased or sewn peasant blouse, gaudy jewelry, and head scarf quickly complete the costume.

THE ROYAL COUPLE
crowned and bejeweled, promenade in rich-looking capes. Her Highness wears a gathered skirt with braid-trimmed sheer overlay. Velvet ribbon woven through lace beading makes quick, elegant cuffs. The king, wearing a short, braid-trimmed gown over knickers, bears the royal scepter.

BAT COSTUMES
must have bat wings to get them flying. Worn over tight clothing, they can be attached with elastic loops. Baby bat's wings are buttoned to her sweat suit. Sew bat ears to headbands, apply face paint, and add some simple accessories.

Metallic fabrics reflect light, making the costume more visible.

SAFETY AND COMFORT

Safety and comfort are important considerations when making a costume. Restrictive or oversized clothing can be uncomfortable and unsafe to wear. Tabard costumes (page 16), however, allow free movement of the arms and legs, and are both comfortable and safe. Long gown costumes (page 30) are easier to walk in if they are hemmed at the anklets. The addition of a belt helps control the fullness of a gown. Full suit costumes (page 36) fit well when they are made from pajama or sweat suit patterns.

Headwear that covers the mouth or nose can make breathing and communicating difficult. Most of all, the wearer of the costume must be able to see clearly and be seen by others. Instead of a mask, face paint can be used to create the desired effect, whilestill allowing maximum range of vision for the wearer.

To increase the safety of trick-or-treat activities after dark, use light-reflective fabrics, such as metallics, whenever possible. Also consider attaching battery-operated lights to a prominent area of the costume for visual impact as well as safety.

Open-faced hoods and face paint allow the wearer clear vision and breathing, unlike masks, which often impair these functions.

Battery-operated lights and chemical-reactive lights can be worn or carried for added safety.

Glow-in-the-dark paints, reflective tapes, and stickers can increase the visibility of a costume.

TABARDS

A primary element of many costumes is a tabard. It consists of front and back panels connected over the shoulders and open at the sides. A ribbon belt secured at the waist keeps the tabard in place while allowing free movement of the arms. Tabards are a great alternative to full suit costumes, as they can be made more quickly with very little consideration to fitting. Simple undergarments are used to complete the basic costume, with the addition of any desired headgear or other accessories.

The surface of the tabard can be embellished in a variety of ways. Shapes, such as the eyes, nose, and mouth of a jack-o'-lantern, can be cut out and appliquéd (page 28) to the front or back of the tabard. Strips of jagged points can be cut from colorful felt and sewn in rows to the surface of the tabard to represent scales or feathers. Insect legs and stingers, or animal tails (page 22) can be sewn and attached to the sides or back of the tabard. Found objects, such as large buttons, metal springs, or egg cartons, can be painted and hand-sewn to the surface of the tabard, to mimic the mechanical riggings of a robot. The possibilities are limited only by the imagination.

It is always a good idea to sketch the costume before drawing the pattern. Determine what other elements to include along with the tabard to complete the costume. If there is a tail, for example, plan to make the back panel of the tabard long enough to allow for its attachment.

Cutting Directions

Cut one tabard front and one tabard back from fabric. Cut one tabard front and one tabard back from lining. Cut one tabard front and one tabard back from ¼" (6 mm) foam.

Cut two 6" (15 cm) pieces of ribbon for the shoulder straps. Cut four 4" (10 cm) pieces of ribbon for the belt loops. Cut a piece of ribbon for the belt, with the length equal to the waist measurements plus 20" (51 cm) for tying.

You Will Need

- paper, for drawing the pattern
- fabric, for front and back panels, and for self-lining, if desired
- interfacing, for lightweight fabrics, optional
- fabric scraps, for appliqués, optional
- lining fabric, for panels that are not self-lined
- ¼" (6 mm) foam, for tabard interlining
- ⅞" (2.2 cm) grosgrain ribbon, in color to match tabard or undergarment

How to Draw a Pattern for a Basic Tabard

1 Sketch desired tabard design. Measure width across shoulders and distance from shoulderAs to desired length of tabard front and back. Draw pattern in desired shape on paper, drawing gentle curve about 1" (2.5 cm) deep at neck. Add ½" (1.3 cm) seam allowance around entire pattern. Cut out pattern.

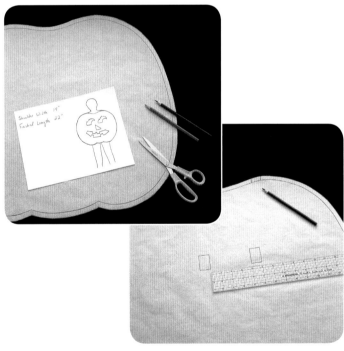

2 Hold pattern up to body. Mark desired positions for shoulder straps. Mark placement for two belt loops at waist level, spaced 3" to 5" (7.5 to 12.5 cm) apart in centers of front and back tabard patterns.

How to Sew a Basic Tabard

1 Apply any surface embellishments that should be done before construction, such as appliqués (page 28). Fold each ribbon for the belt loops in half; stitch ½" (1.3 cm) from cut ends. Press seam allowances open; press each loop flat, with seam centered.

2 Pin belt loops, seam side down, to right side of tabard front and back lining pieces at marks. Stitch loops to lining along upper and lower folds of loops.

3 Pin shoulder straps to right side of tabard front at marks, aligning raw edges; baste. If legs are desired, make legs (page 22) and baste to right side of tabard front along outer edge.

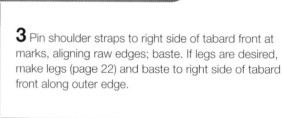

4 Place tabard front over lining, right sides together; layer, lining side down, over the foam. Pin. Stitch ½" (1.3 cm) from raw edges around the entire tabard, leaving opening between shoulder strap marks for turning. Stitch lining to the foam between marks, stitching scant ½" (1.3 cm) from edges.

5 Trim foam close to stitching; trim remaining seam allowances to ¼" (6 mm). Turn the tabard right side out; press.

6 Fold in ½" (1.3 cm) seam allowances of opening; hand-stitch closed. Topstitch ½" (1.3 cm) from the outer edge of tabard. Stitch design lines as desired, avoiding belt loops.

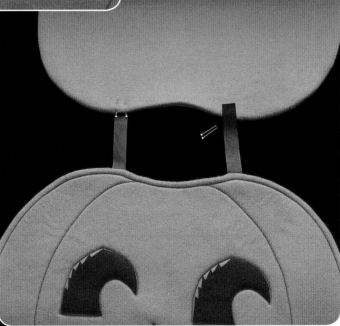

7 Repeat steps 4 and 5 for tabard back. Insert ends of shoulder straps at least ¾" (2 cm) into opening of tabard back at marks; pin. Check fit. Follow step 6, leaving straps pinned in place until they are caught in topstitching.

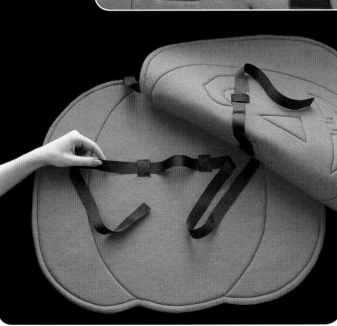

8 Attach any surface embellishments desired. Insert belt through belt loops.

DESIGN-BLOCKED TABARDS

Often it is desirable to construct the tabard from two or more fabrics, sewn together in a pieced design. For example, a tabard for a bumblebee costume would be made of pieced strips of black and yellow fabric. In the same way, a dragon tabard might have a breastplate of one fabric surrounded by another fabric for the main body. These effects are easily achieved, using a method called design blocking. Patterns are drawn for each block of the tabard design. The parts are first sewn together to make the front and back tabard panels. Then the tabard is completed following the instructions for a basic tabard.

How to Draw a Pattern for a Design-blocked Tabard

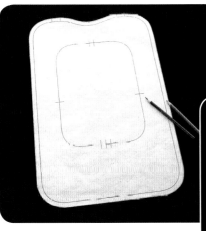

1 Follow the directions for drawing a pattern for a basic tabard on page 17, steps 1 and 2. Draw lines on pattern dividing it into desired design blocks. Mark matching guides across lines that divide blocks.

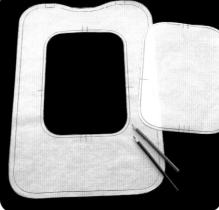

2 Trace each design block separately onto tracing paper; transfer matching guide marks. Add ¼" (6 mm) seam allowances along lines that do not already have seam allowances.

Cutting Directions

Cut one piece of the desired fabric for each of the design blocks in the pieced tabard panels, using the patterns as drawn, in steps 1 and 2. Cut interfacing, if desired.

Cut one tabard front and one tabard back from the lining. Cut one tabard front and one tabard back from the ¼" (6 mm) foam.

Cut two 6" (15 cm) pieces of ribbon for the shoulder straps. Cut four 4" (10 cm) pieces of ribbon for the belt loops. Cut a piece of ribbon for the belt, with the length equal to the waist measurement plus 20" (51 cm) for tying.

You Will Need

- paper, for drawing the pattern
- fabric, for each component of the front and back panels, and for self-lining, if desired
- interfacing, optional
- lining fabric, for panels that are not self-lined
- ¼" (6 mm) foam, for tabard interlining
- ⅞" (2.2 cm) grosgrain ribbon, in color to match tabard or undergarment

How to Sew a Design-blocked Tabard

1 Apply interfacing, if desired, following manufacturer's directions. Staystitch and clip edges as necessary. Pin two adjoining blocks together, matching the guide marks. Stitch ¼" (6 mm) from edges. Press flat. Repeat for all blocks until entire tabard panel has been pieced together.

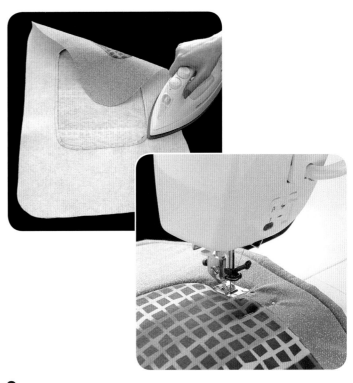

2 Complete tabard as on pages 18 and 19, steps 1 to 8. When stitching design lines in step 6, also stitch in the ditches of the seams between design blocks.

LEGS, TAILS, AND STINGERS

Make a costume look more lifelike by adding a tail, extra legs, or even a stinger. Sew a long, thin tail with an optional contrasting tip or a thicker, padded tail with spikes, suitable for a dragon or dinosaur. Make jointed legs for insect costumes, with wire inserts, allowing them to be bent and shaped. Make a striped bee stinger to add impact to a bumblebee tabard.

Tails and stingers can be sewn to the back of a tabard or full suit costume. To support the weight of a heavy tail on a tabard, a narrow, thin board, such as a ruler, can be inserted into a pocket sewn to the underside of the back panel.

Legs can be sewn into the seam at the outer edge of a tabard or into the side seams of a full suit costume. To help support the outer edge of a tabard with legs, heavy wire can be sewn around the outer edge, as on page 90, steps 3 and 4, before turning the tabard right side out.

Narrow tail with a contrasting tip (opposite) is suitable for many animal costumes. Jointed, bendable legs and a stinger, made from strip-pieced fabric, complete the bee tabard. Two layers of felt were fused together before the spikes for the dragon tail (above) were cut out.

Cutting Directions

Cut a 5" (12.5 cm) strip of fabric and a 5" (12.5 cm) strip of foam for each leg, with the length equal to the desired finished length plus 1" (2.5 cm). Multiply the cut length of one strip by the number of legs plus one; cut a piece of cording with this length.

For a narrow tail, cut a 5" (12.5 cm) strip of fabric and a 5" (12.5 cm) strip of foam, with the length equal to the desired finished length of the tail plus 1" (2.5 cm).

For a narrow tail with a contrasting tip, cut a 5" (12.5 cm) strip of fabric, with the length equal to the desired finished length minus 1" (2.5 cm). Cut a 3" × 5" (7.5 × 12.5 cm) rectangle of contrasting plush felt or synthetic fur for the tip. Cut a 5" (12.5 cm) strip of foam in-terlining, with the length equal to the desired finished length of the tail plus 1" (2.5 cm). Cut a piece of cording, with the length equal to twice the finished length of the tail.

For a shaped tail or stinger, cut two pieces of fabric and two pieces of foam interlining, using the pattern as drawn on page 26, step 1. For a tail with spikes, cut one piece from felt or fused felt, using the pattern as drawn on page 26, step 2.

You Will Need

- fabric
- plush felt or fur, for contrasting tip on narrow tail
- felt or fused felt, for shaped tail with spikes
- ¼" (6 mm) foam, for interlining
- silicone lubricant, for ease in sewing over foam, optional
- ½" (1.3 cm) cording, for narrow tail or legs
- 19-gauge wire, available at hardware stores, for legs or wired narrow tail
- polyester fiberfill, for shaped tail or stinger

How to Sew Legs

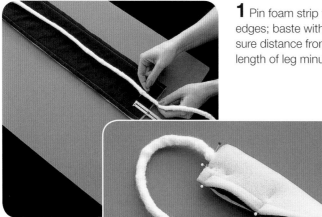

1 Pin foam strip to wrong side of fabric strip on long edges; baste within ½" (1.3 cm) seam allowance. Measure distance from one end of cording equal to cut length of leg minus 1½" (3.8 cm); mark.

2 Fold strip over cording, right sides together, placing one end of strip at mark on cording and extending fabric away from short end of cord. Pin long edges of fabric, matching raw edges.

3 Stitch ½" (1.3 cm) from long raw edges, taking care not to catch cording in stitches and stitching toward short end of cord. Pivot, and stitch across fabric strip, ½" (1.3 cm) from end of strip, centering cording.

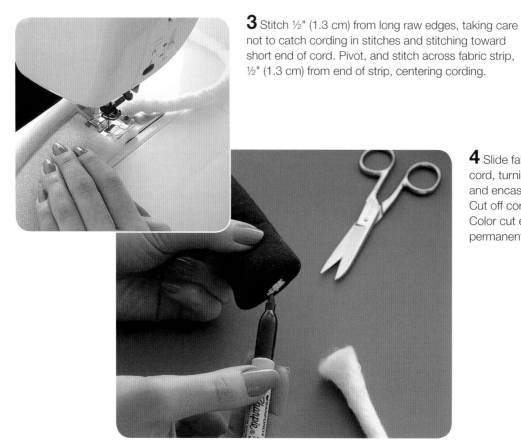

4 Slide fabric onto short end of cord, turning fabric right side out and encasing cording inside strip. Cut off cording at stitched end. Color cut end of cording with permanent marker, if necessary.

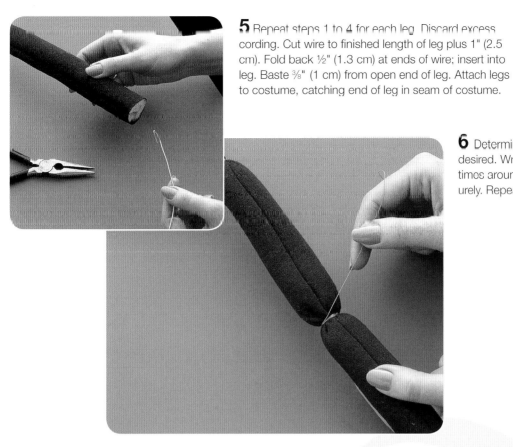

5 Repeat steps 1 to 4 for each leg. Discard excess cording. Cut wire to finished length of leg plus 1" (2.5 cm). Fold back ½" (1.3 cm) at ends of wire; insert into leg. Baste ⅜" (1 cm) from open end of leg. Attach legs to costume, catching end of leg in seam of costume.

6 Determine locations of joints, if desired. Wrap heavy thread several times around log at joint; knot securely. Repeat for all joints.

How to Sew a Narrow Tail

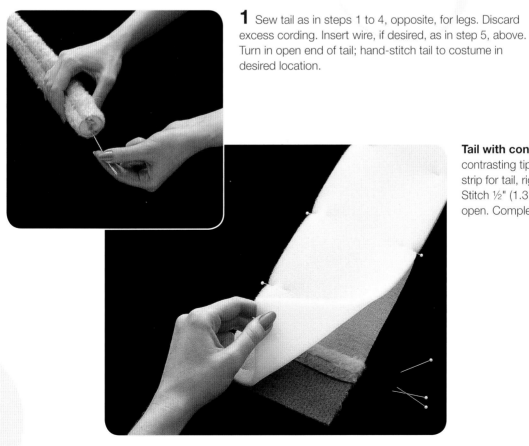

1 Sew tail as in steps 1 to 4, opposite, for legs. Discard excess cording. Insert wire, if desired, as in step 5, above. Turn in open end of tail; hand-stitch tail to costume in desired location.

Tail with contrasting tip. Pin contrasting tip to one end of fabric strip for tail, right sides together. Stitch ½" (1.3 cm) seam; press open. Complete as in step 1, left.

How to Sew a Shaped Tail or Stinger

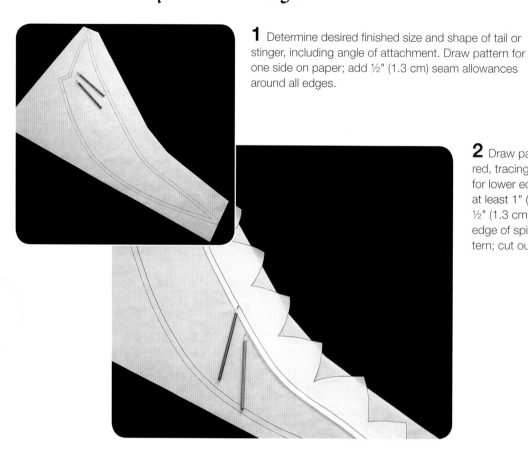

1 Determine desired finished size and shape of tail or stinger, including angle of attachment. Draw pattern for one side on paper; add ½" (1.3 cm) seam allowances around all edges.

2 Draw pattern for spikes, if desired, tracing upper seamline of tail for lower edge of spikes; end spikes at least 1" (2.5 cm) from tail tip. Add ½" (1.3 cm) seam allowance to lower edge of spike pattern. Cut out pattern; cut out spikes.

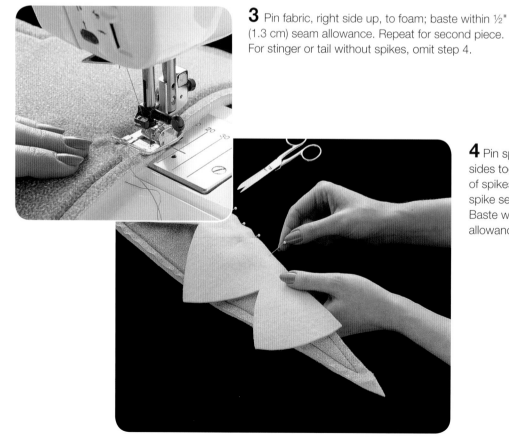

3 Pin fabric, right side up, to foam; baste within ½" (1.3 cm) seam allowance. Repeat for second piece. For stinger or tail without spikes, omit step 4.

4 Pin spikes to one tail piece, right sides together, matching lower edge of spikes to upper edge of tail; clip spike seam allowance as necessary. Baste within ½" (1.3 cm) seam allowance.

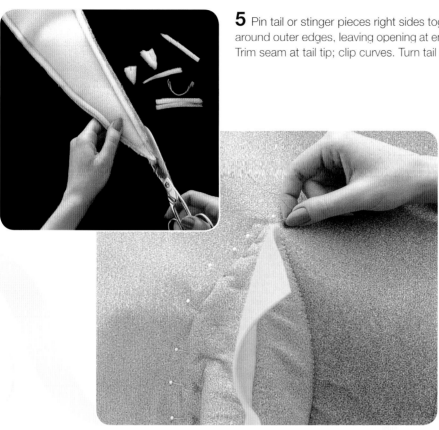

5 Pin tail or stinger pieces right sides together. Stitch around outer edges, leaving opening at end of attachment. Trim seam at tail tip; clip curves. Turn tail right side out.

6 Stuff tail or stinger lightly with polyester fiberfill, if desired. Turn in opening edges. Hand-stitch tail to back of costume in desired location.

Tail Support on Tabard

1 Cut thin wooden support to measure about 2" × 12" (5 × 30.5 cm), or use a wooden ruler. Cut felt pocket 1" (2.5 cm) larger than support.

2 Pin pocket to underside of back panel of tabard, extending above and below the location of the tail attachment. Hand-stitch pocket to tabard along sides and lower edge. Slide support into pocket.

RAW-EDGE APPLIQUÉS

Raw-edge appliqués are an easy way to add patches of color or design features to costume parts, such as a tabard, gown, wings, or a hat. A paper-backed fusible web is used to affix the fabric shapes to the costume surface. For durability, a simple straight stitch is applied around the outer edges of the shapes.

How to Sew Raw-edge Appliqués

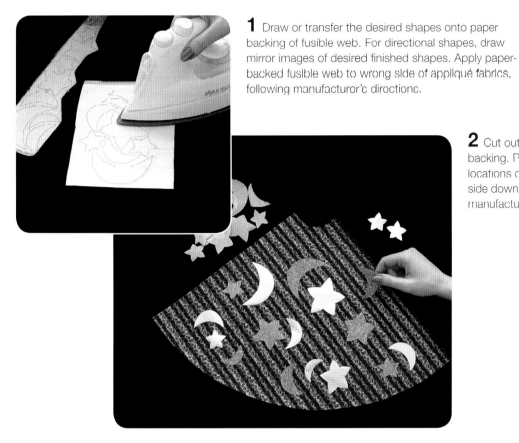

1 Draw or transfer the desired shapes onto paper backing of fusible web. For directional shapes, draw mirror images of desired finished shapes. Apply paper-backed fusible web to wrong side of appliqué fabrics, following manufacturer's directions.

2 Cut out shapes. Remove paper backing. Position shapes in desired locations on costume fabric, fusible side down. Fuse shapes, following manufacturer's directions.

3 Stitch around each shape, ⅛" (3 mm) from raw edges, using short-to-medium-length straight stitch.

Layered appliqués. Follow step 1 for all shapes of the design. Follow steps 2 and 3 for the first layer of shapes. Repeat steps 2 and 3 for each succeeding layer of shapes.

GOWNS

Various Halloween costumes begin with a gown. A simple, loose-fitting gown can be sewn in any size desired, without using a pattern. The fabric is folded, marked, and cut according to the individual's body measurements.

Several sleeve styles can be used, depending on the look desired. You may select wide, sweeping sleeves for a wizard costume; full, gathered sleeves for an angel or princess costume; or long, narrow sleeves for a witch. The gown is cut as one piece, with the width of the fabric running from sleeve hem to sleeve hem. Follow the instructions opposite to determine the yardage needed.

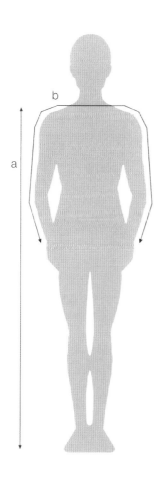

Determining Yardage

Measure (a) from the shoulder to the desired finished length of the gown; add 1" (2.5 cm) for the hem allowance. Multiply this measurement by 2 to determine the cut length needed. Position arms down at the sides of the body; measure (b) from one wrist up the arm, across the back of the shoulders, and down the other arm to the wrist. Add 2" (5 cm) for sleeve hems. Allow at least 2" (5 cm) of extra length for gathered sleeves. If the fabric is wide enough to include the full sleeve length, purchase the fabric yardage determined in measurement (a), above. If the fabric is not wide enough to include the full sleeve length, purchase enough additional fabric to equal the desired circumference of the sleeve at the hem plus 1" (2.5 cm) for seam allowances.

How to Sew a Simple Gown

1 Pin sleeve extensions, if needed, to sides of long fabric piece, right sides together, matching centers of pieces. Sew ½" (1.3 cm) seams. Press seams toward sleeve extensions. Fold entire fabric piece in half crosswise, right sides together, and again, lengthwise. Lay on flat surface.

BASE OF NECK
CIRCUMFERENCE = 13.5"

13.5 ÷ 6.28 = 2.15"

Cutting Directions

Cut the fabric with the length and width equal to the measurements determined above. If additional fabric is needed for the sleeve length, cut two sleeve extensions, with the length equal to the desired finished circumference of the sleeve hem plus 1" (2.5 cm), and the width equal to half of the total additional width needed plus 2" (5 cm) for hem and seam allowances.

You Will Need

• fabric; if possible, select fabric with width that equals or exceeds total arm length
• single-fold bias tape, in color to match fabric
• ⅜" (1 cm) elastic, for gowns with gathered sleeves

2 Measure around the base of neck at the desired neckline placement; divide by 6.28. Draw an arc with a radius of this measurement from the folded center point. Cut on the marked line. Cut a 4" (10 cm) slit from neckline down center back. Cut slit deeper to accommodate wing harness (page 91), if necessary. Cut neck opening ½" (1.3 cm) deeper at front.

(Continued)

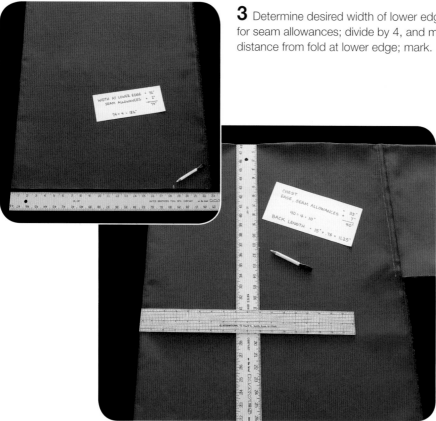

3 Determine desired width of lower edge plus 2" (5 cm) for seam allowances; divide by 4, and measure this distance from fold at lower edge; mark.

4 Measure the chest. Add 6" to 10" (15 to 25.5 cm) for ease and seam allowances; divide by 4. Lay a ruler parallel to the center fold, a distance from the fold equal to this measurement. Measure the back length from the base of the neck to the waist; multiply this measurement by 0.75. Mark point for the underarm along the ruler, a distance from upper fold equal to this measurement.

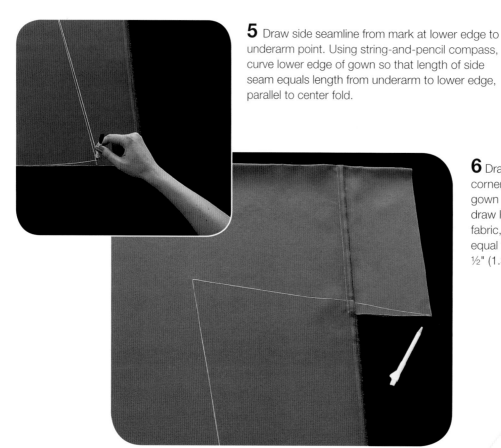

5 Draw side seamline from mark at lower edge to underarm point. Using string-and-pencil compass, curve lower edge of gown so that length of side seam equals length from underarm to lower edge, parallel to center fold.

6 Draw line from underarm to lower corner of the sleeve extension. For gown without sleeve extensions, draw line to point on outer edge of fabric, a distance from upper fold equal to desired sleeve depth plus ½" (1.3 cm).

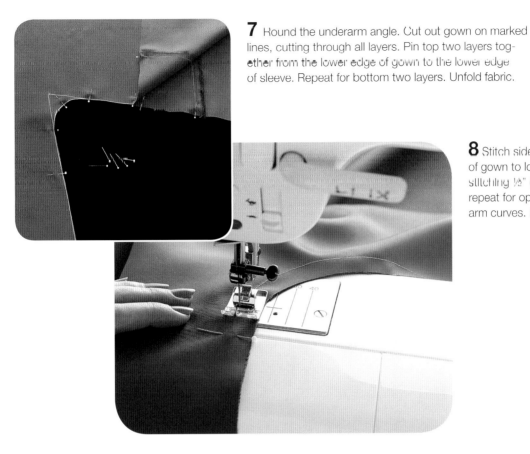

7 Round the underarm angle. Cut out gown on marked lines, cutting through all layers. Pin top two layers together from the lower edge of gown to the lower edge of sleeve. Repeat for bottom two layers. Unfold fabric.

8 Stitch side seam from lower edge of gown to lower edge of sleeve, stitching ½" (1.3 cm) from cut edges; repeat for opposite side. Clip underarm curves. Finish seams, if desired.

9 Open out one folded edge of bias tape; align the edge of slit to the edge of tape, right sides up, with the end of tape at top of neckline. Set machine for short stitch length. Stitch scant ¼" (6 mm) seam, tapering inward to a point just below slit; stop with needle in fabric.

10 Continue stitching up opposite side of slit to the neckline. Cut the tape even with neckline.

(Continued)

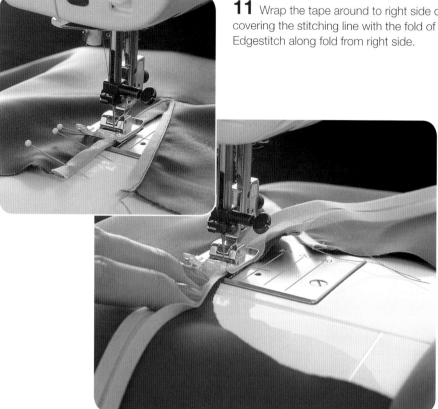

11 Wrap the tape around to right side of gown, just covering the stitching line with the fold of tape; pin. Edgestitch along fold from right side.

12 Open out one folded edge of bias tape; align edge of tape to neckline edge at one side of opening, right side of tape to wrong side of neckline, leaving 10" (25.5 cm) tail of tape for tying. Stitch along the foldline of tape to opposite side of neckline opening; cut tape, leaving 10" (25.5 cm) tail.

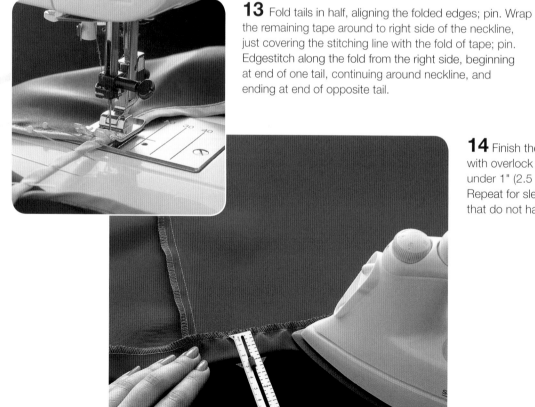

13 Fold tails in half, aligning the folded edges; pin. Wrap the remaining tape around to right side of the neckline, just covering the stitching line with the fold of tape; pin. Edgestitch along the fold from the right side, beginning at end of one tail, continuing around neckline, and ending at end of opposite tail.

14 Finish the lower edge of gown with overlock or zigzag stitch. Press under 1" (2.5 cm) for hem; stitch. Repeat for sleeve hems, for gowns that do not have gathered sleeves.

How to Sew a Gown with Gathered Sleeves

1 Sew the gown as on pages 31 to 34, steps 1 to 14. Press under ½" (1.3 cm) twice on lower edge of the sleeve. Stitch close to the first fold, leaving opening for inserting the elastic.

2 Cut elastic, with length equal to the wrist measurement plus 1" (2.5 cm). Thread elastic through the casing, using a safety pin or bodkin. Try on gown, and mark elastic for a comfortable fit around wrist.

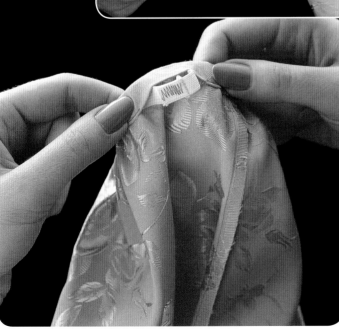

3 Cut the elastic to desired length plus ½" (1.3 cm). Overlap ends of elastic ½" (1.3 cm). Stitch back and forth through both layers, using wide zigzag stitch or three-step zigzag stitch. Ease elastic back into casing. Stitch casing opening closed.

FULL SUIT COSTUMES

Full suit costumes can be made in any style desired, using a commercial pattern for a one-piece pajama or jumpsuit, or a two-piece sweat suit. The pattern may have a hood, or a separate padded hood (page 54) can be made. For infants and toddlers, the pattern may include feet. If the pattern does not have feet, the costume can be designed with separate spats (page 112), if desired, or an attached shoe flap can be added at the bottom of the leg front.

Design inserts can be sewn to the costume for added details, such as a furry back or a soft tummy patch. These inserts are made from fabric that does not ravel, such as felt or synthetic fur. To reduce bulk, the costume fabric is cut away from behind the insert.

How to Sew a Costume with a Design Insert

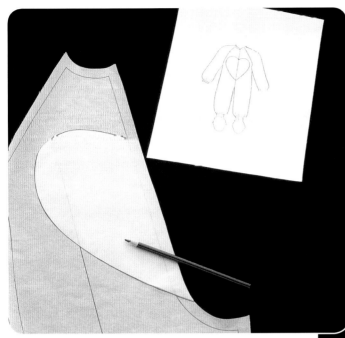

1 Draw sketch of desired finished costume. Place tracing paper over pattern in desired area for design insert. Draw outline of insert; cut out insert pattern. Mark placement of insert on costume pattern. Cut costume and inserts from fabric.

2 Place insert over costume piece in desired location; pin. Stitch close to outer edge of insert. Trim away costume fabric from behind insert. Complete costume, following pattern instructions.

Cutting Directions

Prepare the pattern for a design insert, if desired, following step 1, above. Prepare the pattern for shoe flaps, if desired, as on page 38, steps 1 to 3. Cut out the costume pieces, using the prepared patterns.

You Will Need

- commercial pattern for one-piece pajama or jumpsuit, or two-piece sweat suit
- tracing paper
- nonraveling fabric, such as felt or synthetic fur, for design insert
- lining for costume with shoe flaps
- ¼" (6 mm) foam, for shoe flap interlining
- ⅜" (1 cm) elastic, for costume with shoe flaps
- notions as listed on pattern envelope

How to Sew a Costume with Shoe Flaps

1 Measure heel from ankle to floor over shoe; measure front of foot from ankle to floor over toe of shoe. Record measurements. Mark leg hemline on back and front patterns. Draw a line 1" (2.5 cm) below hemline on back pattern for elastic casing; draw a line 1" (2.5 cm) above hemline on front pattern.

2 Tape rectangle of tracing paper over front pattern, using removable tape; align upper edge of paper to the line drawn in step 1. Extend the side seamlines a distance from hemline equal to heel measurement, as determined in step 1.

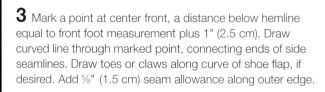

3 Mark a point at center front, a distance below hemline equal to front foot measurement plus 1" (2.5 cm). Draw curved line through marked point, connecting ends of side seamlines. Draw toes or claws along curve of shoe flap, if desired. Add ⅝" (1.5 cm) seam allowance along outer edge.

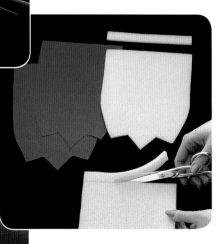

4 Cut out costume pieces. Remove the extension from front pattern piece; cut two pieces from lining and two from foam, using pattern extension. Trim ¾" (2 cm) from upper edges of foam pieces.

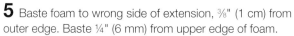

5 Baste foam to wrong side of extension, ⅜" (1 cm) from outer edge. Baste ¼" (6 mm) from upper edge of foam.

6 Press under ¼" (6 mm) at the lower edge of back leg; press under ¾" (2 cm) again, for casing. Open upper fold of casing. Pin front to back, right sides together. Stitch side and inseams, stopping at upper foldline of back leg casing.

7 Press under ¼" (6 mm) for the casing at upper edge of lining. Pin the lining to shoe flap, right sides together. Stitch outer edge of shoe flap, beginning and ending at the hemline. On one side, open folds and stitch lining casing to back casing; press seams open.

8 Trim the foam close to stitching. Trim seam allowance to ¼" (6 mm) along the curve. Clip corners. Turn right side out. Topstitch ¼" (6 mm) from outer edge of shoe flap.

9 Refold casing. Stitch upper edge of casing close to fold. Stitch lower edge of front casing ⅝" (1.5 cm) below first stitching line. Insert elastic through opening at seam; adjust for comfortable fit. Stitch securely.

10 Determine desired position and length for elastic strap to hold the shoe flap in place over shoe; mark. Stitch elastic to shoe flap. Complete costume, following pattern instructions.

Headwear

WITCH HATS

A witch's black hat, with a tall pointed crown and a wide, floppy brim, can set the mood for the rest of the costume. To give the hat more character, the pointed crown can be crumpled and bent. The edge of the brim is wired, allowing the wearer to shape it in dramatic curves.

How to Draw a Pattern for a Witch Hat

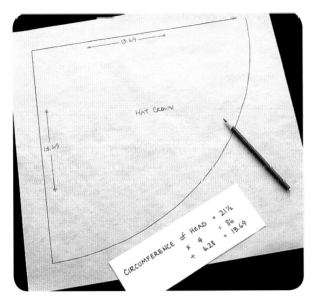

1 Measure the circumference of the head loosely, just above the ears. Multiply this measurement by 4 and divide the answer by 6.28. Draw a quarter-circle with this radius, for the crown of the hat. Straight edges are center back of crown.

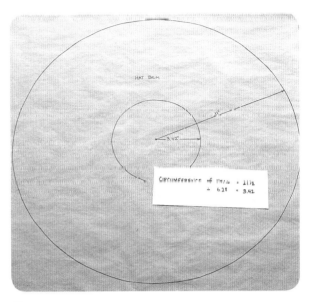

2 Divide the head circumference measurement by 6.28 to determine the radius of the inner brim. Draw a circle with this radius. Draw another circle from the same center point with a radius of 11" (28 cm).

Cutting Directions

Cut one crown, one brim, and one brim lining from the fabric, following the pattern as drawn on this page, in steps 1 to 3. Cut one crown and one brim from interfacing.

You Will Need

- 1⅛ yd. (1.05 m) black fabric, at least 45" (115 cm) wide
- 1⅛ yd. (1.05 m) medium-weight fusible interfacing
- heavy-gauge milliner's wire, available in fabric stores, or 19-gauge wire, available at hardware stores
- grosgrain ribbon, 1" (2.5 cm) wide, with length equal to circumference of head plus 2" (5 cm)
- heavy-gauge chenille stem
- plastic spider; invisible thread

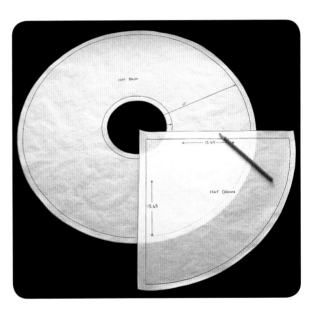

3 Add ½" (1.3 cm) seam allowances to all curved edges. Add ¾" (2 cm) seam allowances to center back edges of the hat crown. Cut out patterns.

How to Sew a Witch Hat

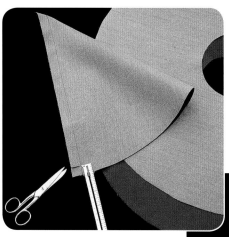

1 Fuse interfacing to crown and brim of hat. Stitch center back seam of crown, right sides together, stitching ¾" (2 cm) from raw edges. Clip seam allowances to stitching line, ⅝" (1.5 cm) above curved edge.

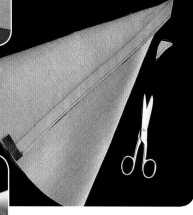

2 Stitch seam allowances together above clip, ⅛" (3 mm) from raw edges; press to one side. Trim seam allowances at point. Press seam allowances open below clip.

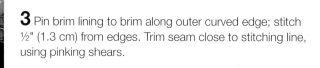

3 Pin brim lining to brim along outer curved edge; stitch ½" (1.3 cm) from edges. Trim seam close to stitching line, using pinking shears.

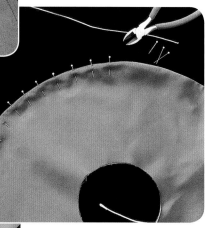

4 Turn brim right side out; press, centering seam along outer edge. Insert milliner's wire between brim and facing, snug against the outer seam; pin in place. Cut wire so ends overlap about 2" (5 cm).

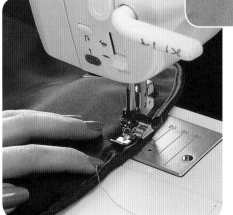

5 Stitch ¼" (6 mm) from outer edge of brim, using zipper foot and encasing wire between stitching line and outer edge.

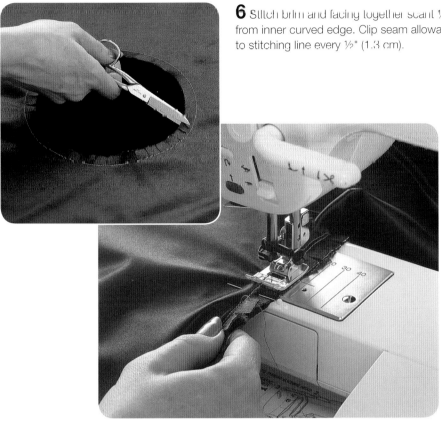

6 Stitch brim and facing together scant ½" (1.3 cm) from inner curved edge. Clip seam allowance close to stitching line every ½" (1.3 cm).

7 Pin brim to crown, right sides together, matching raw edges; stitch ½" (1.3 cm) seam.

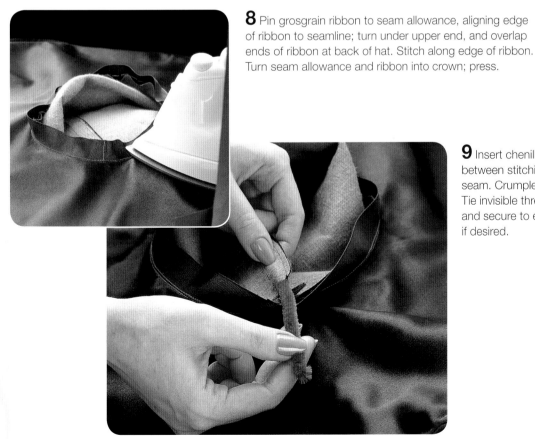

8 Pin grosgrain ribbon to seam allowance, aligning edge of ribbon to seamline; turn under upper end, and overlap ends of ribbon at back of hat. Stitch along edge of ribbon. Turn seam allowance and ribbon into crown; press.

9 Insert chenille stem into space between stitching lines on crown seam. Crumple crown as desired. Tie invisible thread around spider and secure to edge of brim, if desired.

MEDIEVAL HATS

Any girl would love to own a medieval lady-in-waiting hat, whether for a Halloween costume party or just for dressing up and having fun.

This style features a long, sheer veil that flows from the top of a tall crown. The brim is made from jumbo cording covered with shimmery gathered fabric for a luxurious look.

The same hat, without the veil, could be used for a wizard costume. For additional embellishment, celestial shapes can be appliquéd to the crown.

How to Sew a Medieval Hat

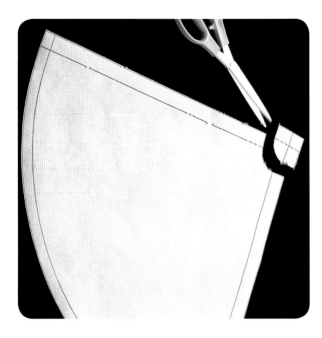

1 Draw a pattern, following steps 1 and 3 at the top of page 43. For hat with veil, draw an arc with radius of 1" (2.5 cm) from point of crown; trim away. For hat without veil, construct crown as on page 44, steps 1 and 2; then continue, beginning with step 6 on page 48.

2 Fuse interfacing to crown of hat. Staystitch ½" (1.3 cm) from upper and lower curves, sewing with short stitches. Clip upper seam allowance to stitching line every ¼" (6 mm).

Cutting Directions

Cut one crown from the fabric, using the pattern as drawn above. Cut a strip of fabric 6" (15 cm) wide from the full width of the crosswire grain of the fabric, for the brim. Cut a piece of jumbo cording, with the length equal to the circumference of the head plus 8" (20.5 cm). Cut one crown from the interfacing.

You Will Need

- ¾ yd. (0.7 m) medium-weight fabric, at least 45 (115 cm) wide, for crown and brim
- ⅝ yd. (0.6 m) medium-weight fusible interfacing.
- 1½" (1.4 m) lightweight sheer fabric, up to 45" (115 cm) wide, for veil
- grosgrain ribbon, 1" (2.5 cm) wide, with length equal to circumference of head plus 2" (5 cm), for hat without veil
- 1 yd. (0.95 m) narrow ribbon, for ties
- jumbo cording
- lighweight cord, such as pearl cotton
- wooden dowel, ¼" (6 mm) in diameter

3 Turn down the upper seam allowance, rolling stitching line to wrong side; press. Stitch ¼" (6 mm) from pressed edge, securing seam allowance to crown.

(Continued)

4 Stitch center back seam of crown, right sides together, stitching ½" (2 cm) from raw edges. Clip seam allowances to stitching line, ⅝" (1.5 cm) above lower curved edge.

5 Stitch seam allowances together above clip to upper edge, ⅛" (3 mm) from raw edges. Pivot, and stitch to seamline, ¼" (6 mm) from top; backstitch to secure. Press seam allowance to one side. Press seam allowances open below clip.

6 Stitch brim strip together into a continuous circle, leaving 3" (7.5 cm) opening at center of seam; press seam allowance open. Divide circle into fourths; mark.

7 Fold circle, wrong sides together, matching raw edges. Zigzag over a cord, stitching ⅜" (1 cm) from the raw edges.

8 Divide lower edge of crown into fourths; mark. Pin brim to crown, right sides together, matching marks; pull up cord to distribute gathers evenly. Stitch ½" (1.3 cm) from raw edge. For hat without veil, follow step 8 on page 45, then steps 12 and 13.

9 Finish one cut edge of veil, overlock or narrow hem. Run two rows of gathering stitches within ½" (1.3 cm) seam allowance on opposite cut edge; divide edge into fourths, and mark.

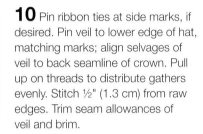

10 Pin ribbon ties at side marks, if desired. Pin veil to lower edge of hat, matching marks; align selvages of veil to back seamline of crown. Pull up on threads to distribute gathers evenly. Stitch ½" (1.3 cm) from raw edges. Trim seam allowances of veil and brim.

11 Turn veil, seam allowances, and ribbon into crown. Pull veil through inside of hat and out hole at top of crown. Edgestitch through crown, seam allowances, and veil, just above the brim, keeping back crown seam allowances free.

12 Cut dowel ¾" (2 cm) shorter than length of center back seam; insert dowel into space between stitching lines on crown seam. Tack opening closed.

13 Wrap ends of jumbo cording with tape. Insert cording through opening in brim; butt ends, and hand-stitch together through tape. Hand-stitch opening closed.

CROWNS AND HALOS

A gleaming crown is important for any royal costume. This style crown is sewn from metallic fabric, padded with thin foam. Sew-on or glue-on gemstones provide a glitzy finishing touch.

A sparkling halo (page 52) is the perfect topper for an adorable angel or fairy. A metallic fabric tubeis stuffed with cording for a soft halo that rests on top of the head. Wired metallic garland or bead trim can be wrapped around the halo, and shimmering streamers of ribbons, beads, or decorative cords can be attached at the back.

How to Sew a Crown

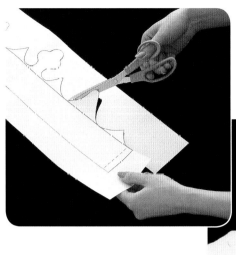

1 Draw rectangle on paper 2½" (6.5 cm) wide, with length equal to circumference of the head plus 2" (5 cm). Draw the desired design above upper long edge of rectangle, beginning and ending design no less than ½" (1.3 cm) from ends of rectangle. Cut out pattern.

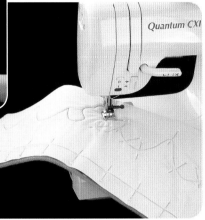

2 Fuse interfacing to wrong side of one fabric rectangle. Transfer crown pattern outline to wrong side of remaining rectangle. Layer fabric, right sides together, over rectangle of foam, with pattern outline on top. Stitch along top line of pattern outline; stitch along bottom line to within 4" (10 cm) of ends.

3 Trim fabric and foam close to stitching. Cut all layers on marked lines at ends. At unstitched sections of lower line, trim fabric to ½" (1.3 cm); trim foam even with line. Clip curves; trim corners.

Cutting Directions

For the crown, cut two rectangles larger than the pattern from fabric, one from interfacing, and one from foam.

For a plain halo, cut one rectangle of fabric, with the length equal to the measurement around the head plus 1" (2.5 cm) and the width equal to the circumference of the cording plus 1" (2.5 cm) for seam allowances.

For a gathered halo, cut one rectangle of fabric, with the length equal to two times the measurement around the head and the width equal to the circumference of the cording plus 1" (2.5 cm) for seam allowances.

You Will Need

Crown:
- tricot-backed metallic fabric
- lightweight fusible interfacing
- foam, ¼" (6 mm) thick
- sew-on or glue-on gemstones

Halo:
- tricot-backed metallic fabric
- cording, ½" (1.3 cm) in diameter
- decorative trims

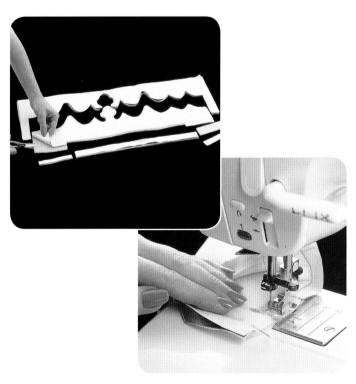

4 Turn right side out. Stitch the ends together ½" (1.3 cm) from the edges, matching seams. Trim the fabric and foam close to stitching. Fold under ½" (1.3 cm) at opening; hand-stitch closed. Stitch or glue gemstones to crown, if desired.

How to Sew a Halo

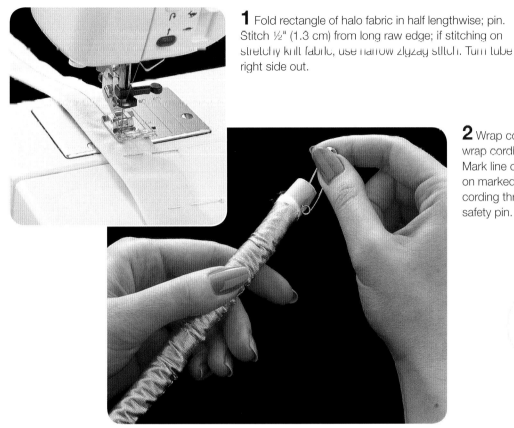

1 Fold rectangle of halo fabric in half lengthwise; pin. Stitch ½" (1.3 cm) from long raw edge; if stitching on stretchy knit fabric, use narrow zigzag stitch. Turn tube right side out.

2 Wrap cording around forehead; wrap cording with tape at overlap. Mark line on tape at overlap; cut on marked line through tape. Insert cording through fabric tube, using a safety pin.

3 Butt the ends of cording; hand-stitch together, stitching through tape. Smooth fabric tube over joined ends; turn under ½" (1.3 cm) on one end of fabric tube, and lap over remaining end. Slipstitch ends of fabric tube together. For gathered halo, distribute gathers evenly.

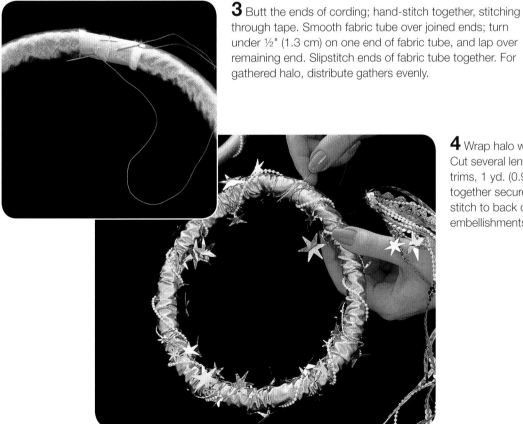

4 Wrap halo with decorative trims. Cut several lengths of ribbons and trims, 1 yd. (0.95 m) long. Stitch trims together securely at center; hand-stitch to back of halo. Add other embellishments as desired.

PADDED HOODS

Create an impressive head for your costume with a padded hood. Foam, sewn between the outer layer and lining, helps support the hood and any other items attached to it. Since it does not cover the face, a padded hood allows for a full range of vision.

Lion manes and features—such as ears, horns, eyes, and antennae—can be attached after completion of the basic hood. During construction, wired flower petals can be sewn around the face opening, and dragon spikes can be sewn into the center top and back seam.

Patterns for two hood styles are given on page 229. The loose-fitting hood—especially effective for animal costumes—can be used for a larger-than-life appearance. For some costumes, such as the zinnia, it is better to have a hood that fits smore snugly. The closer fit helps support the flower petals around the face.

How to Sew a Padded Hood

1 Place the tracing paper over a 1" (2.5 cm) grid. Draw full-size pattern for hood, using the half-size pattern on page 229 as a guide. Cut fabric, lining, and foam pieces. Transfer mark for end of casing to hood.

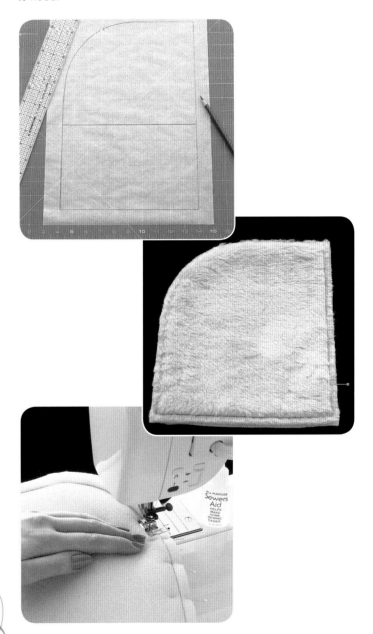

Cutting Directions

Draw the pattern for the hood, as in step 1. Measure over the head to the desired length for the hood; divide this measurement by two, and add 1" (2.5 cm) for seam allowances. Adjust the pattern length, if necessary. Cut two pieces from the fabric, two pieces from the lining, and two pieces from the foam interlining. Cut a rectangle of fabric, 2" × 4" (5 × 10 cm), for the closure underlap.

For a hood with petals, draw a pattern as on page 80, planning nine petals to fit around the hood opening, between marked dots, plus one petal that will be attached under the chin. Cut twenty pieces from the fabric; cut ten pieces from the foam.

You Will Need

- fabric, for hood
- matching or contrasting fabric, for lining
- foam, ¼" (6 mm) thick, for interlining
- hook and loop tape
- drawstring cording
- materials for ears, horns, eyes, or antennae as on page 61, if desired
- macramé cording; 10" (25.5 cm) cardboard template, for hood with lion mane
- felt, for hood with dragon spikes
- fabric; foam, ¼" (6 mm) thick; 19-gauge wire or heavy-gauge milliner's wire, for hood with petals
- silicone lubricant, for ease in sewing over foam, optional

2 Pin the hood piece, right side up, to the foam piece; baste ⅜" (1 cm) from raw edges. Repeat for the remaining piece.

3 Stitch hood pieces, right sides together, along top and center back, stitching ½" (1.3 cm) from raw edges. Trim seam allowances to ¼" (6 mm). Apply silicone lubricant under presser foot and on bed of machine, if desired, to help foam feed evenly.

(Continued)

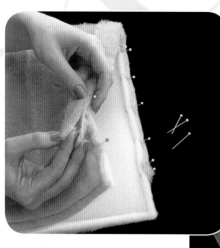

4 Cut 2" (5 cm) strip of fabric for casing, with length equal to the front opening between marks plus 1" (2.5 cm). Fold under ½" (1.3 cm) on ends of casing strip; fold strip in half lengthwise. Pin strip around front opening of hood between marks. Baste casing to hood ⅜" (1 cm) from raw edges.

5 Fold closure underlap piece in half crosswise; stitch ¼" (6 mm) seams along edges perpendicular to fold. Turn right side out; press. Pin to left side of hood, right sides together, just under casing. Baste ⅜" (1 cm) from raw edges.

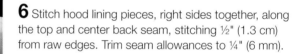

6 Stitch hood lining pieces, right sides together, along the top and center back seam, stitching ½" (1.3 cm) from raw edges. Trim seam allowances to ¼" (6 mm).

7 Pin hood to lining, right sides together, around front and bottom edges. Stitch ½" (1.3 cm) from raw edges, leaving an opening at bottom for turning. Trim seam allowances; clip corners. Turn right side out; press lightly. Slipstitch opening closed. Topstitch along lower edge.

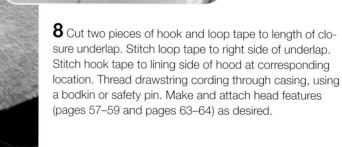

8 Cut two pieces of hook and loop tape to length of closure underlap. Stitch loop tape to right side of underlap. Stitch hook tape to lining side of hood at corresponding location. Thread drawstring cording through casing, using a bodkin or safety pin. Make and attach head features (pages 57–59 and pages 63–64) as desired.

How to Make a Hood with a Lion Mane

1 Cut macrame cording to the desired length for mane base plus 1" (2.5 cm); wrap tape around both ends. Wrap additional macramé cording around cardboard template. Cut wrapped cording at both ends to make 10" (25.5 cm) strands.

2 Center several strands over base, beginning ½" (1.3 cm) from end; pack the strands together densely. Stitch strands to base, using closely spaced, three-step zigzag stitch.

3 Continue stitching strands to base until entire base is covered. Pin mane to hood at placement line. Stitch the mane to the hood, using straight stitch and stitching over the previous stitches. Ravel strands of cording.

How to Make a Hood with Dragon Spikes

1 Follow steps 1 and 2 on page 55. Draw pattern for spikes, tracing curved seamline of hood for lower edge of spikes; begin and end spikes ⅛" (3 mm) from ends of seamline. Cut out spikes.

2 Pin the spikes to the curved edge of the hood, right sides together; clip spike seam allowance as necessary. Baste spikes to hood, within ½" (1.3 cm) seam allowance. Complete the hood as on pages 55–56, steps 3 to 8.

How to Make a Hood with Petals

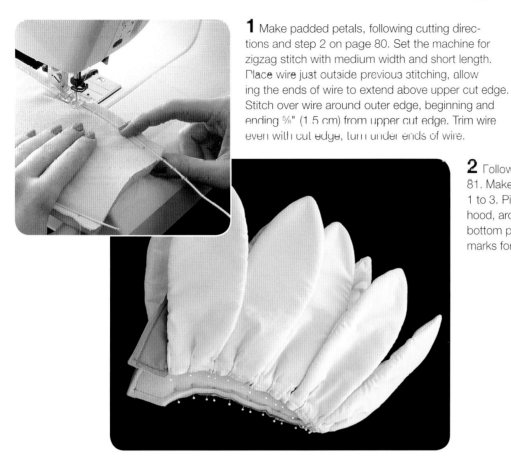

1 Make padded petals, following cutting directions and step 2 on page 80. Set the machine for zigzag stitch with medium width and short length. Place wire just outside previous stitching, allowing the ends of wire to extend above upper cut edge. Stitch over wire around outer edge, beginning and ending ⅝" (1.5 cm) from upper cut edge. Trim wire even with cut edge, turn under ends of wire.

2 Follow steps 3 and 4 on page 81. Make hood as on page 55, steps 1 to 3. Pin nine petals to right side of hood, around the face opening, with bottom petals ¼" (6 mm) from marks for ends of casing; baste.

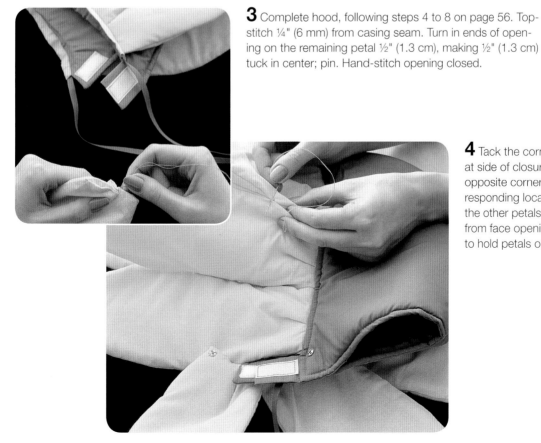

3 Complete hood, following steps 4 to 8 on page 56. Top-stitch ¼" (6 mm) from casing seam. Turn in ends of opening on the remaining petal ½" (1.3 cm), making ½" (1.3 cm) tuck in center; pin. Hand-stitch opening closed.

4 Tack the corner of petal to hood at side of closure; sew snap to opposite corner of petal and corresponding location on hood. Tack the other petals together 2" (5 cm) from face opening. Bend wires to hold petals out from face.

SIMPLE HEADGEAR

Make simple headgear from a purchased headband or ball cap. Cover the headband with fabric, and attach ears, horns, or antennae. Use basic ball caps to top off an animal, bird, or insect costume. Remove the bill from the cap, or leave the bill attached to represent the nose or beak, covering it with felt. For stiffness, fuse two layers of felt together before cutting. Attach ears, horns, eyes, or antennae to either style.

Patterns for horns and two ear styles are provided on page 228. Large glossy eyes can be made from two-piece plastic ball ornaments. Wire notebook springs or large chenille stems work well for antennae. For added whimsy and to cover sharp points, Styrofoam balls or table tennis balls can be attached to the ends.

How to Cover a Headband with Fabric

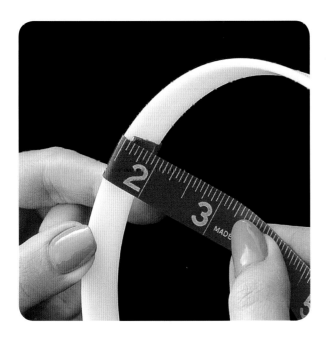

1 Measure circumference at widest point of the headband; cut strip of fabric, with width equal to the determined measurement plus ½" (1.3 cm) and length equal to length of headband plus ½" (1.3 cm).

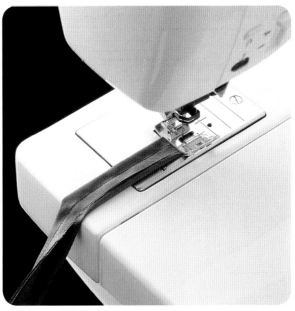

2 Fold strip in half lengthwise; stitch ¼" (6 mm) from long raw edges. Center seam on one side of tube; stitch ¼" (6 mm) seam across one end. Clip corners. Turn right side out.

You Will Need

- headband; fabric for covering headband
- fabric, for horns or ears
- ball cap, in desired color; felt or fused felt, for cap with nose or beak
- fabric; foam, ¼" (6 mm) thick; lining, interfacing, optional, for ears
- fabric; foam ¼" (6 mm) thick; polyester fiberfill, for horns
- two-piece plastic ball ornament; spray adhesive and glitter, or craft acrylic paint; paper clip; pliers; heat source; fused fabric; glue, for eyes
- two jumbo chenille stems, or one wire notebook spring; two small Styrofoam balls or table tennis balls; paint; hot glue, for antennae

3 Insert headband into tube. Turn in ¼" (6 mm) on the open end of tube. Hand-stitch opening closed. Attach ears, horns, or antennae to headband as desired.

How to Make a Headpiece from a Ball Cap

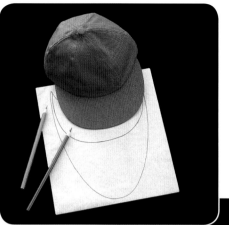

1 **With brim.** Trace outer edge of brim on paper. Draw pattern for nose or beak, extending side edges slightly and curving front edge of brim as desired.

2 Cut two brim extensions from felt; glue extensions to the top and underside of brim, gluing extensions together beyond outer edge of brim. Attach ears, horns, eyes, or antennae as desired.

Without brim. Remove stitches securing brim to cap; remove brim. Restitch the facing to the front of cap. Attach ears, horns, eyes, or antennae as desired.

How to Sew Ears

1 Trace desired pattern from page 228. Cut two pieces from fabric, two from lining, and two from interfacing, if desired; cut two pieces from foam for padded ears. Apply interfacing to the wrong side of ear pieces, if desired, following manufacturer's directions.

2 Pin ear and lining right sides together; for padded ear, layer ear pieces over foam. Stitch ¼" (6 mm) from raw edges, leaving opening along straight edge. Trim foam from seam allowance and ¼" (6 mm) from opening edge.

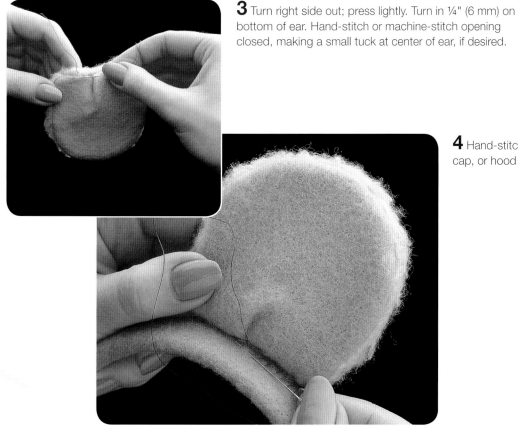

3 Turn right side out; press lightly. Turn in ¼" (6 mm) on bottom of ear. Hand-stitch or machine-stitch opening closed, making a small tuck at center of ear, if desired.

4 Hand-stitch ear to headband, ball cap, or hood at desired location.

How to Sew Horns

1 Trace pattern from page 228. Cut four pieces from fabric and four pieces from foam. Pin fabric, right side up, to foam; baste scant ¼" (6 mm) from raw edges.

2 Pin two horn pieces right sides together. Stitch ¼" (6 mm) from side edges. Trim seam at point; trim foam from opening edge. Turn horn right side out. Repeat for remaining pieces.

3 Stuff the horns with polyester fiberfill, if desired. Turn under ¼" (6 mm) around bottom of horns. Hand-stitch horns to headband, ball cap, or hood at the desired location.

How to Make Large Glossy Eyes

1 Spray inside of plastic ball halves with light coat of spray adhesive; sprinkle with glitter. Or paint the inside of the plastic ball halves as desired; allow to dry. Trim plastic hanger from ball, using mat knife or wire cutter.

2 Straighten one fold of paper clip. Grasp paper clip with pliers; heat end of wire over flame until metal is discolored. Insert end of wire into plastic ball about ⅛" (3 mm) from edge. Reheat paper clip and repeat two or three times, spacing holes evenly around edge of ball.

3 Hand-stitch eye to costume at holes. Cut strips of fused fabric to desired length and width for the eyelids. Cut slashes along one side to make eyelashes, if desired; curl lashes with pencil. Secure eyelids to edge of eye, using glue.

How to Make Antennae

1 Make indentation in Styrofoam balls, using pencil, or poke small hole in table tennis balls, using awl. Paint the balls as desired. Insert chenille stems or notebook springs into balls; secure with hot glue.

Securing stems to cap or hood.
Poke the stem through cap or hood to wrong side. Bend stem at desired length; turn under ¼" (6 mm) at end of stem. Hand-stitch to inside of cap or hood.

Securing stems to the headband. Wrap end of the stem around the headband; twist around base of antenna at top of headband to secure.

1 Securing springs to cap or hood. Cut springs slightly longer than desired finished length, using wire cutter. Poke springs through cap or hood to wrong side. Rotate spring until two turns of spring are inside headgear; compress end of spring.

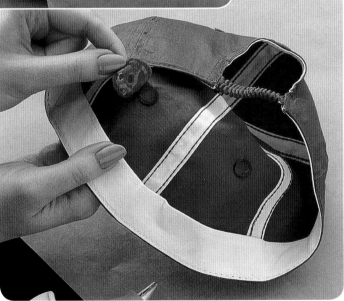

2 Cut two 1" (2.5 cm) felt circles. Secure circles over ends of springs, using generous amount of hot glue; allow to cool. Hand-stitch circles to the inside of cap or hood.

Capes, Skirts, and Wings

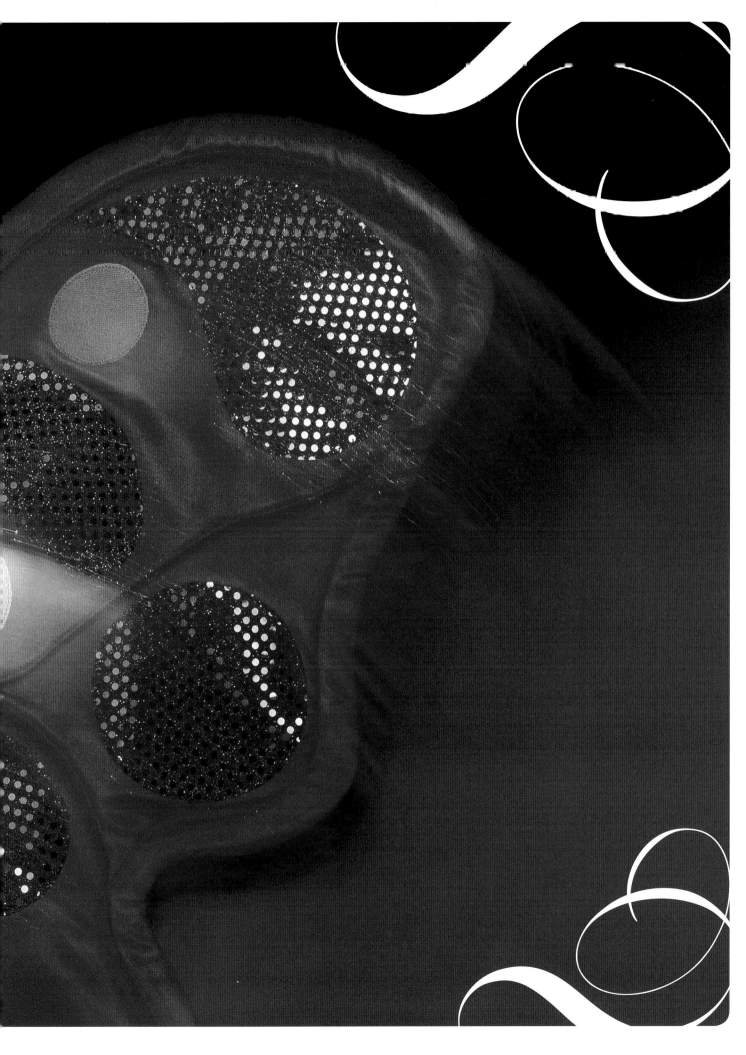

CAPES

A cape is a theatrical and very versatile costume element. Distinguished royalty, wizards and magicians, and even witches can benefit from the use of a cape.

In its simplest form, a cape is a circle of fabric, cut out and tied at the neck, and open down the front. An impressive lined cape can be made, using any stable fabrics for the outer surface and the contrasting lining. When cost and time are factors, an inexpensive cape can be made with minimal sewing, using felt. Either cape style can be made with or without a collar, and both are secured at the neck with ribbon ties.

The length of either cape style can be varied, depending on the desired look; fabric can be pieced to acquire a circle with the necessary diameter. However, to avoid piecing the felt, the circle diameter must be equal to or less than 72" (1.8 m).

Cutting Directions

For a lined cape, cut a square of fabric from the outer cape fabric and the lining fabric twice the desired length of the cape plus about 4" (10 cm). Piece two fabric widths together, if necessary. For the collar, cut one rectangle from the outer cape fabric and one from the lining, as on page 72, step 1.

For a felt cape, cut a square of fabric from felt twice the desired length of the cape plus about 3" (7.5 cm). For the collar, cut one rectangle from felt as on page 74, step 1.

You Will Need

Lined Cape:
- fabric for cape and lining, amount depending on length of cape
- 1 yd. (0.95 m) ribbon, for ties
- interfacing, for collar

Felt Cape:
- felt, amount depending on length of cape
- single-fold bias tape
- 1 yd. (0.95 m) ribbon, for ties

Felt cape without a collar is a quick and easy way to make a cape fit for a king. The magician's cape (opposite) is fully lined and sports a stand-up collar for a more elaborate effect.

How to Sew a Lined Cape

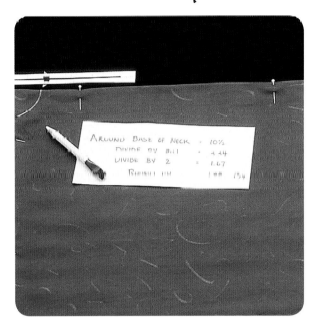

1 Cape with a collar. Fold square of fabric for cape in half lengthwise, then crosswise. Pin layers together. Measure around base of neck. Divide measurement by 3.14; then divide result by 2 to find the radius. Mark an arc on fabric, for neck opening, measuring from folded center of fabric a distance equal to radius, using straight-edge and pencil.

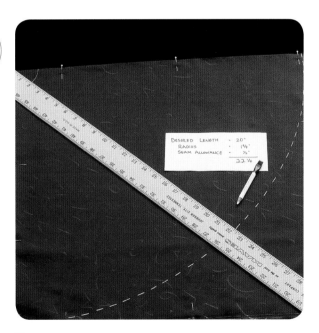

2 Mark an arc for lower edge of cape, measuring from folded center of fabric a distance equal to the desired length of cape plus measurement of radius determined in step 1, plus ½" (1.3 cm) for seam allowance at lower edge.

(Continued)

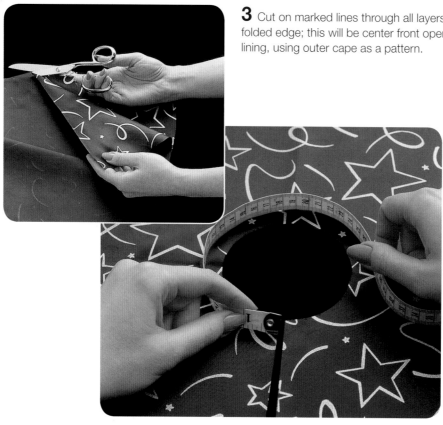

3 Cut on marked lines through all layers. Cut along one folded edge; this will be center front opening of cape. Cut lining, using outer cape as a pattern.

4 Measure the distance around the neck edge of cape from center front to center front, ½" (1.3 cm) from the neck edge. Cut rectangle for the collar from outer fabric and lining, measuring this length by desired width; collar width, not including ½" (1.3 cm) seam allowances, can range from 2½" to 4" (6.5 to 10 cm).

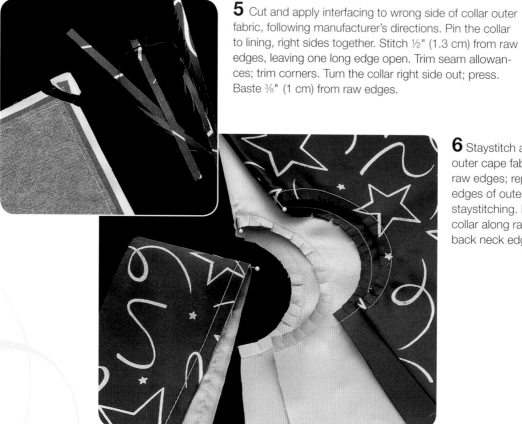

5 Cut and apply interfacing to wrong side of collar outer fabric, following manufacturer's directions. Pin the collar to lining, right sides together. Stitch ½" (1.3 cm) from raw edges, leaving one long edge open. Trim seam allowances; trim corners. Turn the collar right side out; press. Baste ⅜" (1 cm) from raw edges.

6 Staystitch around neck edge of outer cape fabric, ⅜" (1 cm) from raw edges; repeat for lining. Clip neck edges of outer cape and lining to staystitching. Pin-mark center of collar along raw edges and center back neck edge of cape and lining.

7 Pin the collar to right side of outer cape along the neck edge, positioning ends of the collar ½" (1.3 cm) from center front edge of the cape and matching pin marks. Stitch collar to cape a scant ½" (1.3 cm) from raw edges.

8 Pin outer cape to the lining, right sides together. Stitch ½" (1.3 cm) from the raw edges, leaving an opening along the neck edge for turning. Trim the corners. Turn the cape right side out; press. Turn under lining neck edge along the opening; stitch opening closed.

9 Cut ribbon for ties to desired length. Turn under ½" (1.3 cm) at one end of each tie; pin ribbon ties to center front at neck edge. Topstitch securely.

How to Sew a Felt Cape

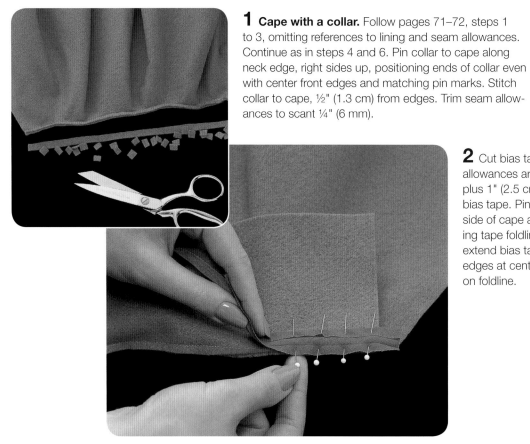

1 Cape with a collar. Follow pages 71–72, steps 1 to 3, omitting references to lining and seam allowances. Continue as in steps 4 and 6. Pin collar to cape along neck edge, right sides up, positioning ends of collar even with center front edges and matching pin marks. Stitch collar to cape, ½" (1.3 cm) from edges. Trim seam allowances to scant ¼" (6 mm).

2 Cut bias tape to length of seam allowances around neck opening plus 1" (2.5 cm). Open one fold of bias tape. Pin bias tape to wrong side of cape along neck edge, aligning tape foldline to stitching line; extend bias tape ¼" (6 mm) beyond edges at center front. Stitch on foldline.

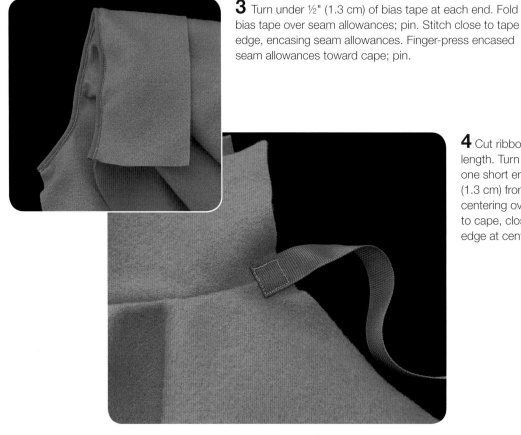

3 Turn under ½" (1.3 cm) of bias tape at each end. Fold bias tape over seam allowances; pin. Stitch close to tape edge, encasing seam allowances. Finger-press encased seam allowances toward cape; pin.

4 Cut ribbon for ties to desired length. Turn under ½" (1.3 cm) on one short end; pin to cape front, ½" (1.3 cm) from edge at center front, centering over neck seam. Stitch tie to cape, close to edges and along edge at center front as shown.

1 Cape without a collar. Follow pages 71–72, steps 1 to 3. Cut bias tape to length of neck opening plus 1" (2.5 cm). Open one fold of bias tape. Pin bias tape to right side of cape around neck edge, aligning raw edges; extend bias tape ½" (1.3 cm) beyond edges at center front. Stitch bias tape to neckline, stitching on foldline.

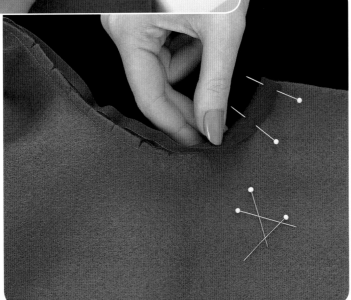

2 Press seam allowances toward bias tape. Clip the neck seam allowances as necessary. Turn under ½" (1.3 cm) of bias tape at each end. Fold bias tape to wrong side of cape; pin. Stitch close to remaining fold in bias tape. Follow step 4, opposite, pinning ties to center front at neck edge.

SKIRTS

Skirts are often a primary costume element. Instructions are given for several basic styles. Choose from an elastic-waist skirt with an optional overlay or a leaf or petal skirt (page 80).

Make the elastic-waist skirt in any length desired, using a fullness of two to four times the waist measurement. To add an overlay, select a fabric that does not ravel, such as tulle, or select a lace with a decorative lower edge. More fullness can be used in the optional overlay, depending on the look desired and the sheerness of the fabric. The skirt overlay can be embellished at the lower edge with sequin trim.

The leaf or petal skirt is constructed with foam for a firm, padded appearance. Design lines can be stitched onto the leaves to create veins.

Cutting Directions

Cut one rectangle from the skirt fabric, with the length equal to the desired length of the skirt plus 1" (2.5 cm) for seam and hem allowances and the width equal to two to four times the waist measurement, depending on the desired fullness of the skirt.

For an overlay with equal fullness to the skirt, cut one rectangle from the overlay fabric, with the length equal to the desired length of the skirt plus ½" (1.3 cm). The cut width of the overlay fabric is equal to the cut width of the skirt fabric. For an overlay with added fullness, the cut length of the overlay fabric is equal to twice the desired skirt length plus 1" (2.5 cm). The cut width of the overlay fabric may be four to six times the waist measurement, depending on the weight of the fabric and the desired look. Seam fabric widths together in ⅜" (1 cm) seams, if necessary.

Cut a strip of skirt fabric for the elastic casing at the waist, with the length equal to the widest hip measurement plus 3" (7.5 cm) and the width equal to two times the width of the elastic plus 1¼" (3 cm).

You Will Need

- fabric, for skirt, amount depending on length and fullness of skirt
- fabric, such as lace or tulle, for overlay, amount depending on length and fullness
- elastic of desired width, for waist
- decorative trim, for lower edge of overlay, optional; amount needed is equal to the cut width of the overlay
- lightweight cord, such as pearl cotton

How to Sew an Elastic-waist Skirt

1 Stitch skirt widths together in ⅜" (1 cm) seams, forming continuous circle. Finish seams with overlock or zigzag stitch. Turn up ¼" (6 mm) twice to wrong side on lower edge of skirt. Stitch close to second fold.

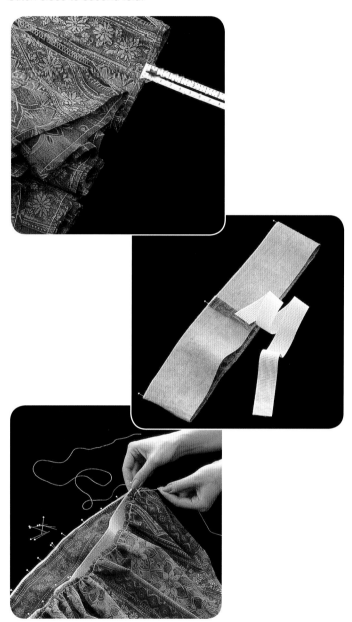

2 Stitch short ends of waistband casing, right sides together, in ½" (1.3 cm) seam, leaving opening for inserting elastic. Press seam allowances open. Finish one long edge of waistband with overlock or zigzag stitch. Divide remaining long edge into quarters; pin-mark.

3 Zigzag over cord ⅜" (1 cm) from upper edge of skirt. Divide upper edge into quarters; pin-mark. Pin unfinished edge of waistband casing to upper edge of skirt, right sides together, matching pin marks. Pull up on cord to gather; distribute fullness evenly.

(Continued)

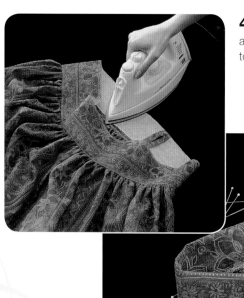

4 Stitch ½" (1.3 cm) from raw edges. Trim seam allowances to ¼" (6 mm). Press seam allowances toward casing.

5 Fold casing to inside, overlapping stitching line ⅜" (1 cm); pin from right side, along the seamline. Stitch on right side of skirt, stitching in the ditch of the casing seam.

6 Cut elastic equal to waist measurement plus 1" (2.5 cm). Thread elastic through casing, using a safety pin or bodkin. Try on skirt, and mark elastic for a comfortable fit around waist. (Skirt is shown inside out, for ease in fitting.)

7 Cut elastic to desired length plus ½" (1.3 cm). Overlap ends of elastic ½" (1.3 cm). Stitch back and forth through both layers, using wide zigzag stitch or three-step zigzag stitch. Ease elastic back into casing. Stitch casing opening closed.

How to Sew a Skirt with an Overlay of Equal Fullness

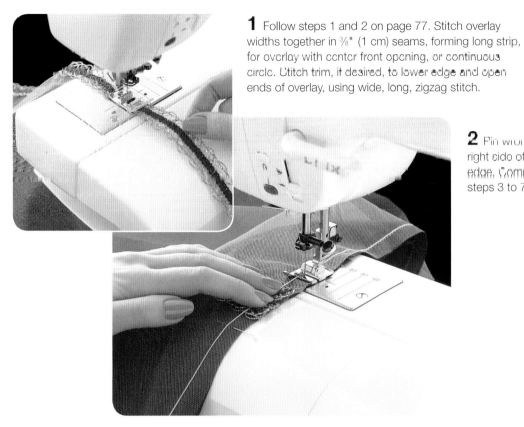

1 Follow steps 1 and 2 on page 77. Stitch overlay widths together in ⅜" (1 cm) seams, forming long strip, for overlay with center front opening, or continuous circle. Stitch trim, if desired, to lower edge and open ends of overlay, using wide, long, zigzag stitch.

2 Pin wrong side of overlay to right side of skirt, along upper edge. Complete skirt, following steps 3 to 7 on pages 77–78.

How to Attach an Overlay with Added Fullness

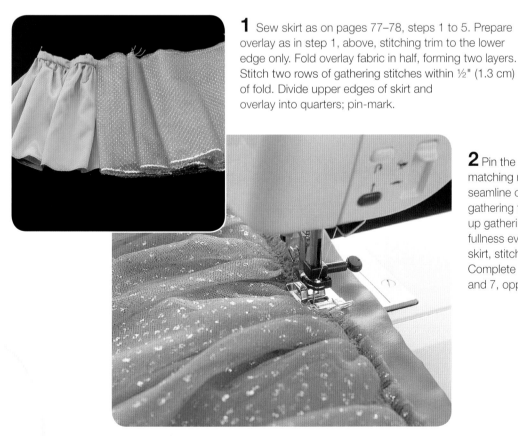

1 Sew skirt as on pages 77–78, steps 1 to 5. Prepare overlay as in step 1, above, stitching trim to the lower edge only. Fold overlay fabric in half, forming two layers. Stitch two rows of gathering stitches within ½" (1.3 cm) of fold. Divide upper edges of skirt and overlay into quarters; pin-mark.

2 Pin the overlay to right side of skirt, matching marks and centering seamline of casing between gathering threads of the overlay. Pull up gathering threads, distributing fullness evenly. Stitch overlay to skirt, stitching over casing seamline. Complete skirt, following steps 6 and 7, opposite.

Leaf or Petal Skirt

Cutting Directions

Cut a 3½" (9 cm) strip of fabric for the waistband, with the length equal to the waist measurement plus 6" (15 cm) for ease, seam allowances, and overlap.

Determine the number and size of the leaves or petals that will fit between the pin marks, as marked in step 1. Draw a pattern for the leaf or petal, with the upper edge 1" (2.5 cm) wider than the desired finished width. Add ½" (1.3 cm) seam allowance around the entire pattern. Cut two pieces from fabric and one from foam, for each leaf or petal.

Wrap the elastic snugly around the waist; mark. Cut the elastic 3" (7.5 cm) longer than the marked length.

You Will Need

- fabric
- ¼" (6 mm) foam, for petal or leaf interlining
- waistband elastic, 1" (2.5 cm) wide
- hook and loop tape

How to Sew a Leaf or Petal Skirt

1 Press up ½" (1.3 cm) on one long edge of waistband. Pin-mark the opposite edge of waistband ½" (1.3 cm) from one end and 2½" (6.5 cm) from opposite end.

WAISTBAND MEASUREMENT = 32"
32" ÷ 8 LEAVES = 4"
+ 1" TUCK
5" UPPER EDGE

2 Layer pieces, right sides together, over the foam. Stitch ½" (1.3 cm) from raw edges, leaving upper edge open.

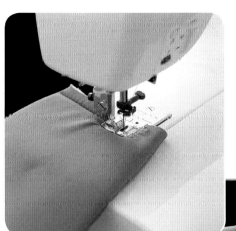

3 Trim seam allowances to scant ¼" (6 mm). Turn leaf or petal right side out; press. Baste upper raw edges together; trim out foam on upper edge.

4 Repeat steps 2 and 3 for all leaves or petals. Stitch any design lines. Fold ½" (1.3 cm) tuck at center of upper edge, folding out 1" (2.5 cm) of fabric; baste.

5 Pin leaves or petals to the edge of the waistband between pin marks, right sides together, matching raw edges; space leaves or petals evenly. Stitch ½" (1.3 cm) seam.

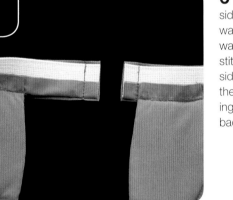

6 Fold waistband in half, right sides together; place elastic over waistband as shown. Stitch across waistband, ½" (1.3 cm) from ends, stitching through elastic. Turn right side out; press. Pin in the ditch of the seam. Stitch in the ditch, catching lower edge of waistband on back side.

7 Cut 2" (5 cm) length of hook and loop tape. Stitch hook side of tape to right side of extension. Stitch loop side of tape to wrong side of waistband at the opposite end.

BAT WINGS

Select from two wing styles to give your bat or alien creature costume a dramatic finish. One wing style is made from fabric and is attached to the arms and legs, using loops of elastic. The other is made from felt and is buttoned to the costume along the lower edge of the sleeve and down the side of the garment. Both wing styles allow ease for stretching the arms outward. Instructions for creating the wing patterns are flexible, so you can adjust the spacing between the scallops along the outer edges of the wings and determine the best placement of elastic loops or buttons for securing the wings in place.

When making the fabric wing, you may wish to place the elastic loops at the wrist, shoulder, thigh, ankle, and a couple of inches to each side of the elbow and knee for ease of movement. For the felt wing, it is not necessary to space all the buttonholes at equal distances from each other. You may wish to space them closer together along the sleeve and upper body and farther apart along the leg. It may also be helpful to space two buttonholes close together at the underarm area to secure the wing close to the garment at this point.

The amount of fabric and ribbon needed for the wings depends on the size of the costume. It may be helpful to make the pattern before selecting the fabric.

Cutting Directions

For fabric wings, cut two pieces for each wing, using the pattern as drawn on pages 84–85, steps 1 to 6.

For felt wings, cut one piece for each wing, using the pattern as drawn on page 85, steps 1 and 2.

You Will Need

Fabric Wings:
- fabric, contrasting fabric may be used for wing back
- elastic, ¼" to ½" (6 mm to 1.3 cm) wide

Felt Wings:
- felt
- ribbon, ⅝" (1.5 cm) wide
- buttons

Metallic brocade fabric is used to make an impressive set of wings for a young bat hero (opposite). Felt wings add fun to the playful bird-creature costume below.

How to Draw the Pattern for Bat Wings

1 Fabric wings. Draw line (a) on paper, with length equal to measurement from underarm to ankle. At ankle end, draw 1¼" (3 cm) line (b) perpendicular to line (a). At underarm end, draw line (c) perpendicular to line (a), with length equal to measurement from underarm to wrist.

2 Draw line (d) from underarm, at 45 degree angle from line (c), with same length as line (c). Draw lines connecting endpoints of lines (b), (c), and (d), for outer edge of wing pattern.

3 Mark point on line (b) ⅝" (1.5 cm) from line (a). Mark another point on upper section of outer edge ⅝" (1.5 cm) from line (d).

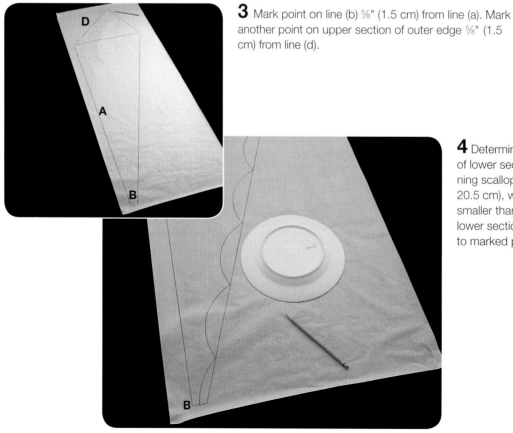

4 Determine desired scallop spacing of lower section of outer edge, planning scallop widths of 6" to 8" (15 to 20.5 cm), with lowest scallop slightly smaller than others. Draw scallops in lower section, drawing lowest scallop to marked point on line (b).

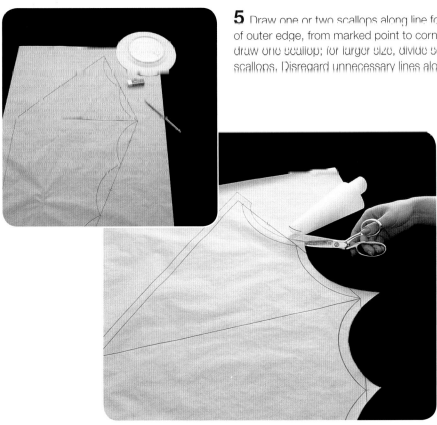

5 Draw one or two scallops along line for upper section of outer edge, from marked point to corner; for small size, draw one scallop; for larger size, divide section into two scallops. Disregard unnecessary lines along outer edge.

6 Add ½" (1.3 cm) seam allowances to all edges of pattern. Cut out pattern.

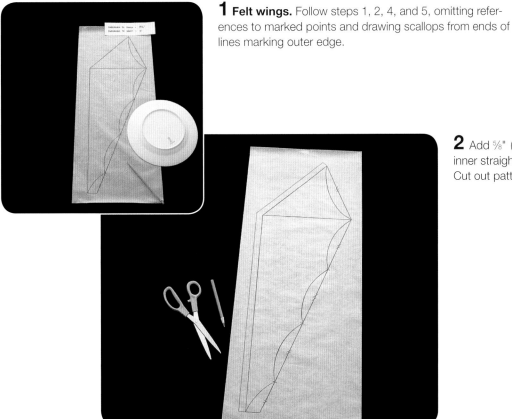

1 Felt wings. Follow steps 1, 2, 4, and 5, omitting references to marked points and drawing scallops from ends of lines marking outer edge.

2 Add ⅝" (1.5 cm) extension along inner straight edge of wing pattern. Cut out pattern.

How to Sew Bat Wings from Fabric

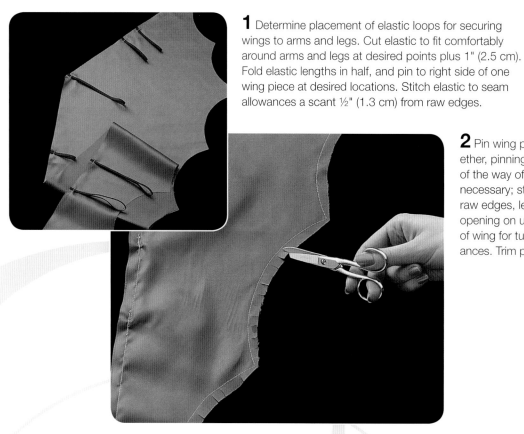

1 Determine placement of elastic loops for securing wings to arms and legs. Cut elastic to fit comfortably around arms and legs at desired points plus 1" (2.5 cm). Fold elastic lengths in half, and pin to right side of one wing piece at desired locations. Stitch elastic to seam allowances a scant ½" (1.3 cm) from raw edges.

2 Pin wing pieces right sides together, pinning elastic loops out of the way of seam allowances, if necessary; stitch ½" (1.3 cm) from raw edges, leaving about 6" (15 cm) opening on underarm-to-ankle side of wing for turning. Trim seam allowances. Trim points, and clip curves.

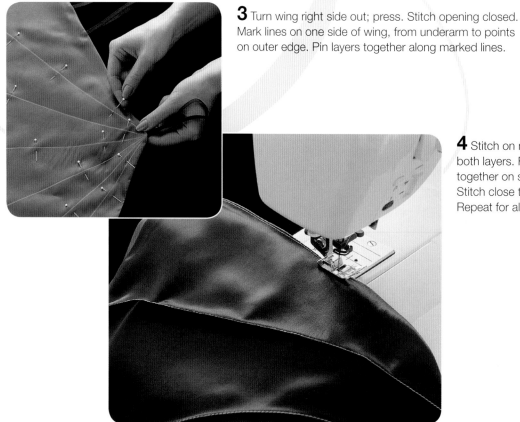

3 Turn wing right side out; press. Stitch opening closed. Mark lines on one side of wing, from underarm to points on outer edge. Pin layers together along marked lines.

4 Stitch on marked lines through both layers. Fold wing front sides together on stitched line; press fold. Stitch close to fold, making pintuck. Repeat for all stitched lines.

How to Sew Bat Wings from Felt

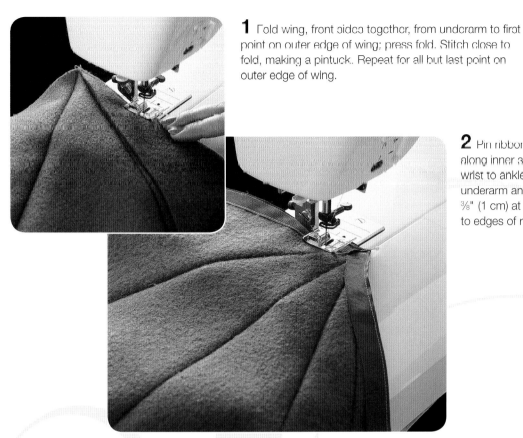

1 Fold wing, front sides together, from underarm to first point on outer edge of wing; press fold. Stitch close to fold, making a pintuck. Repeat for all but last point on outer edge of wing.

2 Pin ribbon to front side of wing, along inner straight edges, from wrist to ankle, pinning a tuck at underarm and turning under about ⅜" (1 cm) at each end. Stitch close to edges of ribbon.

3 Mark placement of buttonholes on ribbon, spacing as necessary to hold wing securely to garment. Make buttonholes.

4 Try on costume; mark button positions. Stitch buttons to costume.

PADDED WINGS

Padded wings can be used for costumes such as angels, birds, butterflies, or other winged creatures. The wings are designed with a layer of foam between layers of fabric. Wire may be stitched around the outer seam allowances to help support the shape of the wings.

To create wings that sparkle, make the wings from fabrics with metallic threads. Or use a base fabric and cover it with a transparent overlay of glitter organza, glitter tulle, or sparkle mesh. Simply pin the overlay pieces, right side up, to the right sides of all the wing pieces, and baste them together ⅜" (1 cm) from the outer edges. Then sew the wings as on pages 90–91, steps 1 to 6. Wings may also be embellished with appliquéd designs, if desired.

Padded wings can be designed in any shape and size to suit the needs of the costume, provided each wing is no wider than the width of the foam. Simply draw a pattern on paper for one wing, to the size and shape desired. For best results, plan to join the wings in a straight center seam at least 6" (15 cm) long. You may use any of the wing designs shown here or develop your own style. Add a ½" (1.3 cm) seam allowance to the entire outer edge of the pattern.

Wings can be worn in a variety of ways. They can be sewn directly to the back of another part of the costume, such as a tabard or full suit. Wings can be made detachable, using hook and loop tape. Or an elastic harness that fits over the shoulders can be sewn to the wings. When worn with a gown, an opening in the back of the gown allows the harness to be hidden.

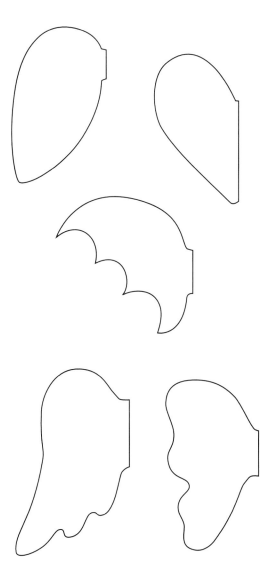

Cutting Directions

Cut four wing pieces, two for the fronts and two for the backs.

For a transparent overlay, cut four wing pieces from transparent fabric.

Cut two wing pieces from ¼" (6 mm) foam. Trim ½" (1.3 cm) seam allowance from center edges.

You Will Need

- fabric, for wings
- fabric, for wing overlay, optional
- foam, ¼" (6 mm) thick, for padded wings
- silicone lubricant, for ease in sewing over foam, optional
- 19-gauge wire, for wings with wired edges
- hook and loop tape, for attaching wings, optional
- elastic, ½" (1.3 cm) wide, for harness

Wings appear in nature and fantasy in a wide range of shapes and sizes. Select a design to suit your costume, or draw a shape, following the guidelines above.

How to Sew Padded Wings

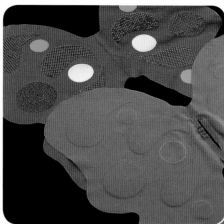

1 Apply any surface embellishments that should be done before construction, such as appliqués (page 28). Pin wing back pieces, right sides together, along center back; stitch ½" (1.3 cm) seam. Press seam allowances open. Repeat for wing front pieces, leaving 6" (15 cm) opening in seam for turning.

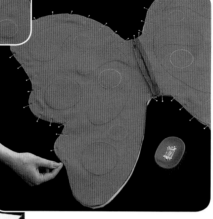

2 Lay foam on flat surface, butting center edges. Place wing front over wing back, right sides together; then place over foam. Pin. Stitch ½" (1.3 cm) from outer edges. Apply silicone lubricant to bed of the machine to help foam feed evenly. For wings without wired edges, omit steps 3 and 4.

3 Set machine for zigzag stitch with medium width and short stitch length. Place the wire just outside previous stitching; stitch over wire around the entire outer edge in a continuous circle, using a 90/14 needle and a presser foot with recessed bottom.

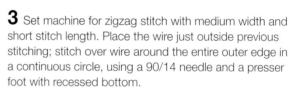

4 Cut the wire, overlapping ends about 2" (5 cm). Zigzag over overlapped ends, using closely spaced stitches to secure.

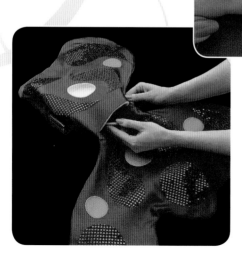

5 Trim seam allowances to ¼" (6 mm). Clip curves and trim points. Turn wings right side out through center front seam opening. Push out points of wings, using the eraser end of a pencil. Press lightly; hand-stitch opening closed.

6 Topstitch around wings 1" (2.5 cm) from outer edges. Stitch any additional design lines. Sew wings to back of costume, or attach elastic harness, see below.

How to Sew an Elastic Harness

1 Wrap the elastic from the center back over one shoulder and return to the center back; pull the elastic comfortably snug. Mark point of intersection.

2 Cut elastic twice the length from end to mark. Overlap the ends ½" (1.3 cm), forming circle. Stitch back and forth through both layers, using wide zigzag stitch or three-step zigzag stitch.

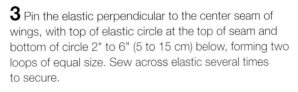

3 Pin the elastic perpendicular to the center seam of wings, with top of elastic circle at the top of seam and bottom of circle 2" to 6" (5 to 15 cm) below, forming two loops of equal size. Sew across elastic several times to secure.

SHEER WINGS

Sheer wings are especially suitable for insect costumes. They can be made from any sheer fabric and are supported with wire around the outer edges. Sheer wings work best when made on a small scale, with each wing measuring no wider than 15" (38 cm) across.

Draw the wings in one large piece, with a flat section between the wings that measures 2" (5 cm) wide and 4" to 6" (10 to 15 cm) long. Keep outer edges gently rounded, avoiding any sharp curves.

How to Sew Sheer Wings

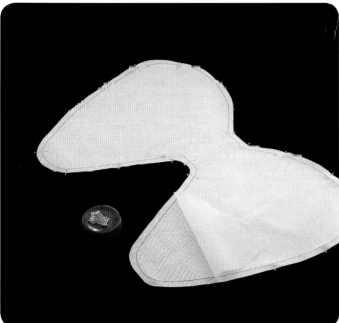

1 Draw the desired shape for wings on tear-away stabilizer or wide paper. Pin sheer fabric over the stabilizer. Cut out both layers, leaving ½" (1.3 cm) margin around outer edge. Pin sheer fabric to stabilizer along entire outer edge.

Cutting Directions

Cut a piece of sheer fabric and a piece of stabilizer as in step 1.

Cut a 4" (10 cm) strip of medium-weight fabric for the center support, with the length equal to twice the length of the center flat section of the wings plus 1" (2.5 cm). Cut a piece of ¼" (6 mm) foam 1⅞" (4.7 cm) wide, with the length equal to the length of the center flat section of the wings.

You Will Need

- tear-away stabilizer or wide paper, such as freezer paper
- 19-gauge wire, available at hardware stores, or heavy-gauge milliner's wire, available at fabric stores
- sheer fabric
- medium-weight fabric, in color to match wings, and ¼" (6 mm) foam, for center support
- elastic, ½" (1.3 cm) wide, for harness, optional
- hook and loop tape, for attaching wings, optional

2 Set machine for zigzag stitch with medium width and short length. Place the wire over fabric along marked line, beginning at center flat section; stitch over wire around entire outer edge in a continuous circle; using presser foot with recessed bottom.

(Continued)

3 Cut wire, overlapping ends about 2" (5 cm). Zigzag over overlapped ends, using closely spaced stitches to secure.

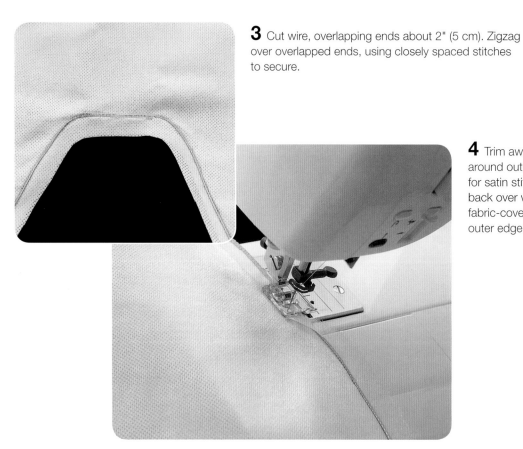

4 Trim away stabilizer carefully around outer edge. Set machine for satin stitch. Turn excess fabric back over wire. Satin stitch over fabric-covered wire around entire outer edge.

5 Trim away excess fabric up to the stitches. Carefully tear away remaining stabilizer.

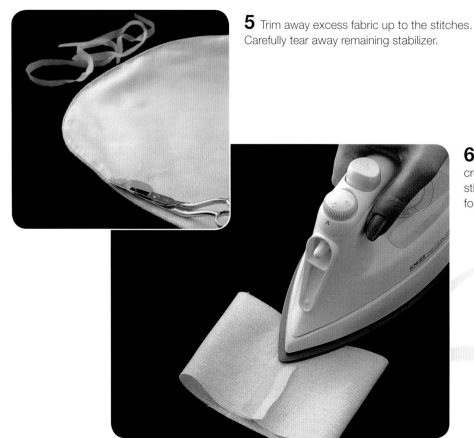

6 Fold cover support strip in half crosswise, right sides together; stitch ½" (1.3 cm) from raw edges, forming circle. Press seam open.

7 Fold in raw edges of support, butting at center; press. Insert foam strip under the folds on side of support opposite seam.

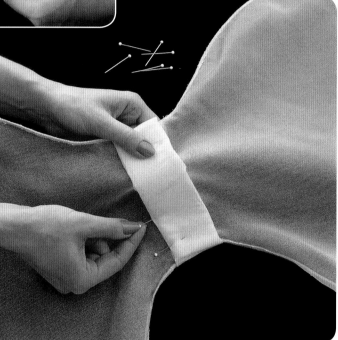

8 Slip one wing through support, and center padded front over flat space between wings. If wings will be worn with elastic harness, prepare the harness as on page 91, steps 1 and 2. Slip harness through back of support; pin, spacing elastic as in step 3. Align front and back outer edges of support; pin.

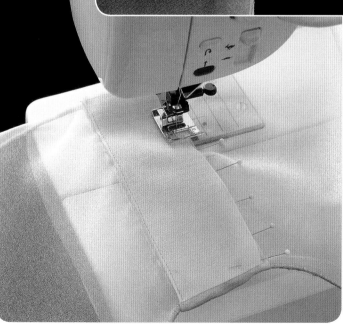

9 Edgestitch along outer edges on front of support, catching back of support and harness, if used, in the stitching. For wings without harness, sew wings to back of costume, or sew hook side of hook and loop tape to back of support; sew loop side of tape to costume.

Finishing
Touches

COLLARS

An imaginative collar can be an expressive costume element. The fabric, shape, and details can be varied to make a collar suitable for any creature or character.

Either of two basic collar styles can be sewn to suit the needs of the costume. A flat collar can be designed with a uniquely shaped outer edge and accented with topstitched design lines, if desired. For added shaping, it can be padded with foam interfacing.

A gathered collar is a suitable accent for a fairy or ballerina costume or for any type of plant costume. For this collar style, use fabrics that do not ravel easily. Nylon knit fabrics or tulle work well.

Padded flat collar, suitable for a superhero, is sewn from metallic fabric and accented with stitched design lines (opposite). The lion's mane is a plush felt flat collar. The fairy wears a frilly, two-layered gathered collar.

How to Draw a Pattern for a Flat Collar

1 Cut rectangle of paper larger than the desired finished size of collar. Fold paper in half lengthwise, then crosswise. Measure neck and mark arc on paper as on page 71, step 1.

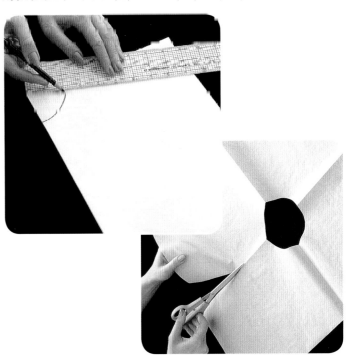

Cutting Directions

For a flat collar, make the pattern as on pages 99 and 100, for steps 1 to 4. Cut two collar pieces from fabric, using the pattern. For a padded flat collar, also cut one collar piece from foam, using the pattern.

For a gathered collar, cut one rectangle from fabric, with the length equal to the measurement of the neck at the base of the neck times three and the width equal to the desired length of the collar plus ½" (1.3 cm). Cut one 2¾" (7 cm) strip for the binding, equal to the length of the neck measurement plus 2" (5 cm), cutting the strip on the bias for woven fabrics or on the crosswise grain for knit fabrics.

You will need

Flat Collar:
• fabric, amount depending on size of collar
• ¼" (6 mm) foam, for padded collar
• hook and eye closure

Gathered Collar:
• fabric, for collar, about one collar length for neck sizes 15" (38 cm) and smaller
• fabric, for binding, about ⅛ yd. (0.15 m) for crosswise grain or about ⅜ yd. (0.35 m) for bias grain
• hook and eye closure

2 Cut out neck opening. Unfold paper; slash on one fold to neck opening, for center back seam.

(Continued)

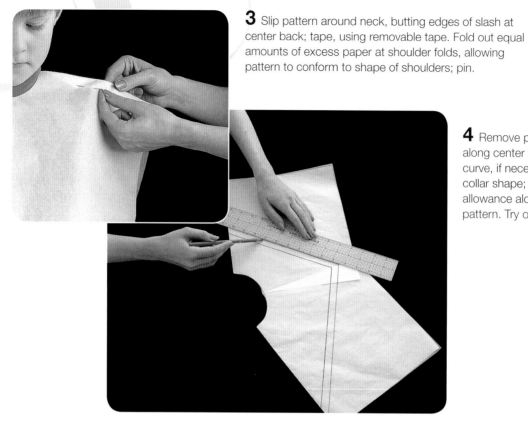

3 Slip pattern around neck, butting edges of slash at center back; tape, using removable tape. Fold out equal amounts of excess paper at shoulder folds, allowing pattern to conform to shape of shoulders; pin.

4 Remove pattern; fold in half along center front. Adjust neckline curve, if necessary. Draw desired collar shape; add ½" (1.3 cm) seam allowance along outer edge. Cut out pattern. Try on pattern to check fit.

How to Sew a Flat Collar

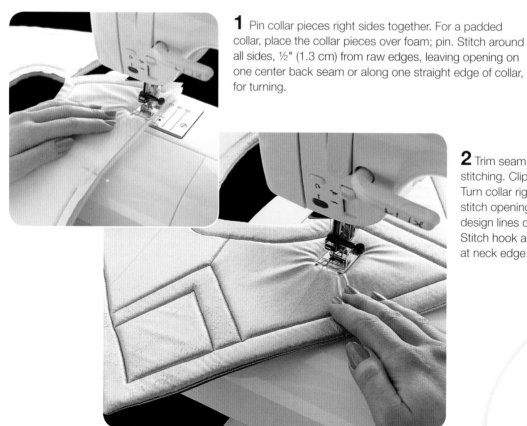

1 Pin collar pieces right sides together. For a padded collar, place the collar pieces over foam; pin. Stitch around all sides, ½" (1.3 cm) from raw edges, leaving opening on one center back seam or along one straight edge of collar, for turning.

2 Trim seam allowances close to stitching. Clip any corners or curves. Turn collar right side out; press. Slip-stitch opening closed. Stitch any design lines on collar as desired. Stitch hook and eye to center back at neck edge.

How to Sew a Gathered Collar

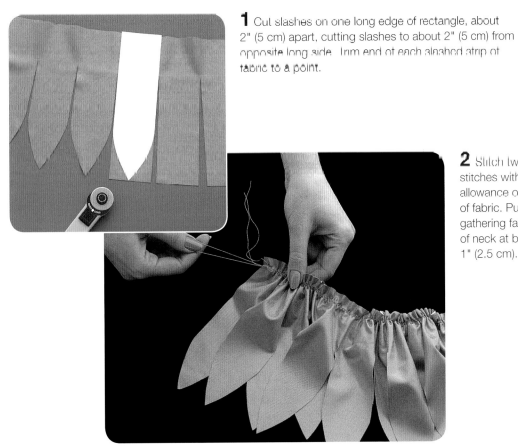

1 Cut slashes on one long edge of rectangle, about 2" (5 cm) apart, cutting slashes to about 2" (5 cm) from opposite long side. Trim end of each slashed strip of fabric to a point.

2 Stitch two rows of gathering stitches within ½" (1.3 cm) seam allowance on remaining long edge of fabric. Pull gathering threads, gathering fabric to measurement of neck at base of neck plus 1" (2.5 cm).

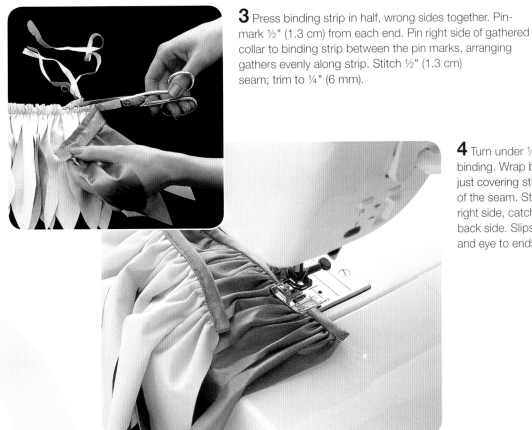

3 Press binding strip in half, wrong sides together. Pin-mark ½" (1.3 cm) from each end. Pin right side of gathered collar to binding strip between the pin marks, arranging gathers evenly along strip. Stitch ½" (1.3 cm) seam; trim to ¼" (6 mm).

4 Turn under ½" (1.3 cm) at ends of binding. Wrap binding to back side, just covering stitching; pin in the ditch of the seam. Stitch in the ditch on the right side, catching the binding on the back side. Slipstitch ends. Stitch hook and eye to ends of collar.

ARM AND LEG ACCENTS

Armbands or gathered wristlets and anklets can give added flourish to simple costumes. Gathered wristlets or anklets can be made to accompany a gathered collar for a fairy princess costume. Or, for any plant costume, they can be made to look like clumps of leaves. Padded armbands, much like spats or hoods, give the costume a larger-than-life appearance. They can be designed with appliqués (page 28) or other surface embellishments to coordinate them with the rest of the costume. Vent hose armbands are a wonderful addition to a robot costume. They are made from flexible vinyl vent hose, which can be purchased at any hardware store in a range of sizes. Select a hose that comfortably fits over the arm. A larger diameter hose can be used to make leggings.

Cutting Directions

For gathered wristlets, cut two strips of fabric, with the length equal to three times the wrist measurement and the width equal to the measurement from the wrist to the knuckles plus ½" (1.3 cm) for seam allowance. Cut two 2¾" (7 cm) bias strips of fabric for the elastic casing, with the length equal to the wrist measurement plus 3" (7.5 cm). Cut two pieces of ¼" (6 mm) elastic, with the length equal to the wrist measurement plus ½" (1.3 cm).

For gathered anklets, cut two strips of fabric, with the length equal to three times the ankle measurement and the width equal to the measurement from the ankle to the floor plus ½" (1.3 cm) for the seam allowance. Cut two 2¾" (7 cm) bias strips of fabric for the elastic casing, with the length equal to the ankle measurement plus 4" (10 cm). Cut two pieces of ¼" (6 mm) elastic, with the length equal to the ankle measurement plus ½" (1.3 cm).

For padded armbands, cut two armbands, two lining pieces, and two pieces of foam interlining, using the pattern drawn on page 105, steps 1 and 2. Cut hook and loop tape, with the length equal to the finished length of the opening minus ¼" (6 mm).

For vent hose armbands or leggings covered with two-way stretch fabric, cut one rectangle of fabric, with the width equal to the measurement around the vent hose and the length equal to the desired length of the armband or legging plus 4" (10 cm). If using tricot-backed lamé, cut one rectangle of fabric, with the width equal to the measurement around the vent hose plus 1" (2.5 cm) for seam allowances and the length equal to the desired length of the armband or legging plus 4" (10 cm).

Gathered wristlets and padded armbands (opposite) complement gathered collars (page 101) and flat, padded collars (page 99). Vent hose armbands and leggings (above) enhance a robot costume.

You Will Need

Gathered Wristlets or Anklets:
- fabric
- ¼" (6 mm) elastic

Padded Armbands:
- fabric
- ¼" (6 mm) foam, for interlining
- hook and loop tape

Vent Hose Armbands or Leggings:
- vinyl vent hose, with diameter large enough to fit over arms or legs
- masking tape
- wire cutter
- metallic two-way stretch fabric, or tricot-backed lamé
- ¼" (6 mm) elastic

How to Sew Gathered Wristlets or Anklets

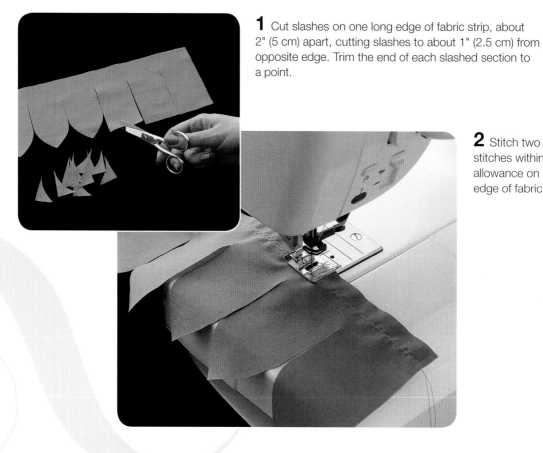

1 Cut slashes on one long edge of fabric strip, about 2" (5 cm) apart, cutting slashes to about 1" (2.5 cm) from opposite edge. Trim the end of each slashed section to a point.

2 Stitch two rows of gathering stitches within ½" (1.3 cm) seam allowance on remaining long edge of fabric.

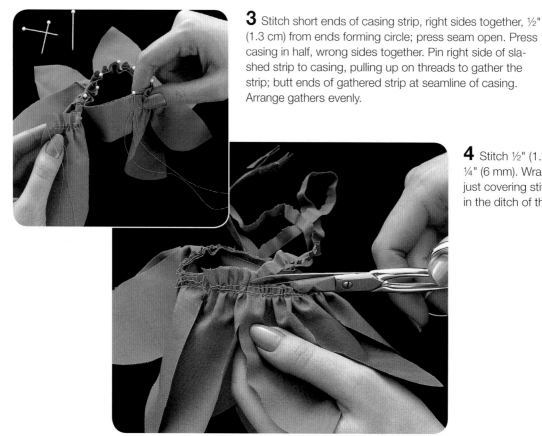

3 Stitch short ends of casing strip, right sides together, ½" (1.3 cm) from ends forming circle; press seam open. Press casing in half, wrong sides together. Pin right side of slashed strip to casing, pulling up on threads to gather the strip; butt ends of gathered strip at seamline of casing. Arrange gathers evenly.

4 Stitch ½" (1.3 cm) seam; trim to ¼" (6 mm). Wrap casing to back side, just covering stitching; pin in the ditch of the seam.

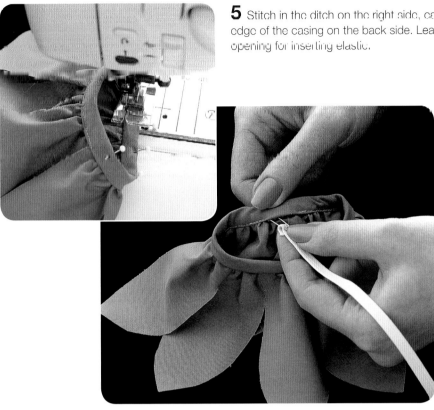

5 Stitch in the ditch on the right side, catching the lower edge of the casing on the back side. Leave 1" (2.5 cm) opening for inserting elastic.

6 Insert elastic through opening, using safety pin. Overlap ends ½" (1.3 cm); stitch securely. Stitch opening closed.

How to Draw a Pattern for Padded Armbands

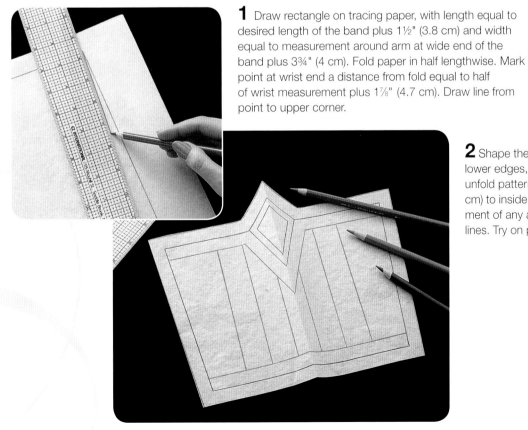

1 Draw rectangle on tracing paper, with length equal to desired length of the band plus 1½" (3.8 cm) and width equal to measurement around arm at wide end of the band plus 3¾" (4 cm). Fold paper in half lengthwise. Mark point at wrist end a distance from fold equal to half of wrist measurement plus 1⅞" (4.7 cm). Draw line from point to upper corner.

2 Shape the pattern at upper and lower edges, if desired. Cut on line; unfold pattern. Draw seamlines ½" (1.3 cm) to inside of cut edges. Mark placement of any appliqués and design lines. Try on pattern to check fit.

How to Sew Padded Armbands

1 Apply any surface embellishments that should be done before construction, such as appliqués (page 28). Pin armband and lining, right sides together, over foam interlining. Stitch ½" (1.3 cm) from raw edges, leaving 3" (7.5 cm) opening for turning.

2 Fold back upper layer at opening; stitch lower layer to foam, scant ½" (1.3 cm) from raw edges. Trim seam allowances; trim corners.

3 Turn armband right side out; press. Slipstitch opening closed. Topstitch along upper and lower edges only. Stitch any design lines on armbands.

4 Pin hook side of tape to outside of armband, close to one opening edge. Pin loop side of tape to inside of armband, close to opposite edge; stitch close to all edges of tape. Repeat for other armband, lapping opening edges in opposite direction.

How to Make Vent Hose Armbands or Leggings

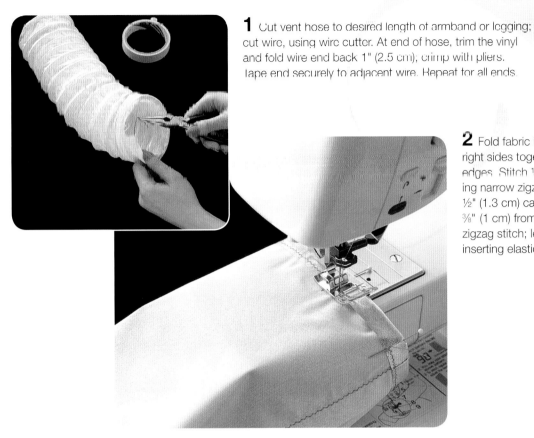

1 Cut vent hose to desired length of armband or legging; cut wire, using wire cutter. At end of hose, trim the vinyl and fold wire end back 1" (2.5 cm), crimp with pliers. Tape end securely to adjacent wire. Repeat for all ends.

2 Fold fabric in half lengthwise, right sides together; pin long edges. Stitch ½" (1.3 cm) seam, using narrow zigzag stitch. Turn under ½" (1.3 cm) casing at ends. Stitch ⅜" (1 cm) from the fold, using narrow zigzag stitch; leave opening for inserting elastic.

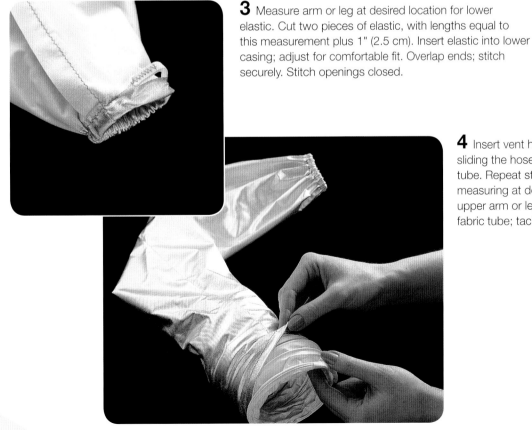

3 Measure arm or leg at desired location for lower elastic. Cut two pieces of elastic, with lengths equal to this measurement plus 1" (2.5 cm). Insert elastic into lower casing; adjust for comfortable fit. Overlap ends; stitch securely. Stitch openings closed.

4 Insert vent hose into fabric tubes, sliding the hose to elasticized end of tube. Repeat step 3 for upper elastic, measuring at desired location on upper arm or leg. Center hose in fabric tube; tack ends in place.

GLOVES

Give the finishing touch to your costume with a pair of custom-designed gloves. Make an animal paw, complete with claws, from an inexpensive work glove. Paint a pair of garden gloves to match a robot or space suit costume. Or simply add long, painted fingernails to plain black nylon or cotton gloves to coordinate with a bat or witch costume.

Begin with an inexpensive pair of gloves, and add stitched or painted embellishments and plastic nail tips as appropriate for your costume. Purchase nail tips in the cosmetics section of drugstores, or find specialty nail tips at costume shops. Follow manufacturers' recommendations and warnings, since nail tip glues will bond to skin in a few seconds. Look for black, brown, green, or glow-in-the-dark fingernail polish to give the nail tips the perfect finish.

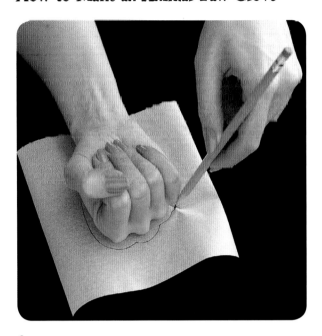

How to Make an Animal Paw Glove

You Will Need

Animal Paws:
• gloves
• plush felt or synthetic fur scraps

Raw-edge Accent:
• ¼" (6 mm) foam
• nonraveling fabric scraps

Padded Fabric Accent:
• fabric scraps
• fusible interfacing
• ¼" (6 mm) foam

Nails or Claws:
• plastic nail tips, in desired length; nail glue
• fingernail polish, of desired color
• wooden dowel, ⅜" to ½" (1 to 1.3 cm) in diameter
• plastic sandwich bag

1 Clench fist, and position on paper as shown. Trace around the fist, eliminating thumb. Cut just inside marked lines to make pattern for fur patch on upper paw. Cut two fur patches, reversing the pattern for one to make a right and left patch.

2 Glue fur patch to top of glove, using fabric glue. Repeat for remaining glove. Apply claws as in steps 1 to 3, on page 111, if desired.

How to Make a Glove with Raw-edge Fabric Accent

1 Cut desired shape from nonraveling fabric to fit over top of glove, using scissors or pinking shears. Cut piece of foam slightly larger than fabric shape. Pin fabric over foam; stitch ¼" (6 mm) from outer edges of fabric.

2 Stitch design lines over padded fabric shape as desired. Trim excess foam close to stitching. Hand-stitch accent to top of glove along outer stitching line. Apply nails or claws if desired.

How to Make a Glove with a Padded Fabric Accent

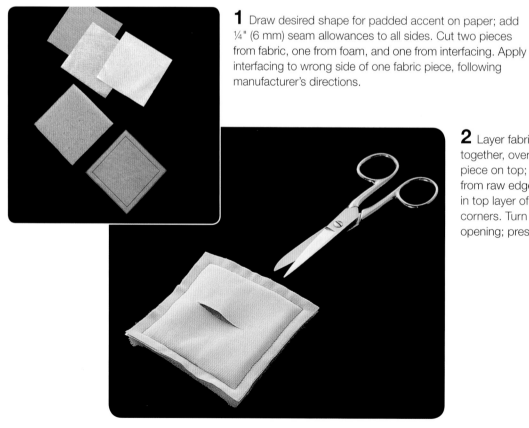

1 Draw desired shape for padded accent on paper; add ¼" (6 mm) seam allowances to all sides. Cut two pieces from fabric, one from foam, and one from interfacing. Apply interfacing to wrong side of one fabric piece, following manufacturer's directions.

2 Layer fabric pieces, right sides together, over foam, with interfaced piece on top; pin. Stitch ¼" (6 mm) from raw edges. Cut small opening in top layer of fabric for turning. Trim corners. Turn right side out through opening; press.

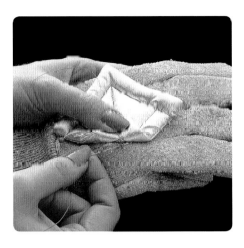

3 Topstitch around outer edges of design. Stitch additional design lines on accent as desired. Hand-stitch accent to top of glove along outer design line. Apply nails or claws as below, if desired.

How to Apply Nails or Claws to Gloves

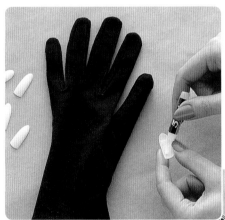

1 Trim nail tips as desired. Wrap the dowel with plastic sandwich bag; insert into thumb of glove. Apply glue liberally to lower half of nail tip.

2 Press nail tip in place over the dowel; hold for about 30 seconds. Move dowel to next finger; apply glue to nail tip, and press in place. Repeat for all nails. Allow nails to dry thoroughly.

3 Apply two or three coats of nail polish to nails, if desired, allowing nails to dry between coats.

SPATS

Padded spats are an effective addition to costumes of all kinds. Worn over shoes, they can be made to look like metallic boots for a robot or an astronaut, or like oversized animal feet and paws. Foam interlining gives the spats enough body to stand up on the leg. A hook-and-loop-tape closure up the back makes them easy to put on and take off, while an elastic strap under the shoe helps to hold them in place.

How to Draw a Pattern for Spats

SHOE SOLE CIRCUMFERENCE = 19 ¾"
+ EASE ___1___"
20 ¾"

20 ¾" ÷ 2 = 10 ⅜"

1 Measure the circumference of shoe sole; add 1" (2.5 cm) for ease, and divide by 2. Draw a line of this length on paper, for lower edge of pattern. Draw a line perpendicular to this line, with the length equal to desired finished length, for back of spat.

SHOE ARCH MEASUREMENT = 8 ¾"
9 ½" ÷ 2 = 4 ¾"   + EASE
___1___"
9 ¾"

Cutting Directions

Draw the pattern as in steps 1 to 5, on this page and the next. Cut four pieces from fabric, four from lining, four from foam, and four from interfacing, if desired, for each pair of spats. Cut two pieces of ¼" (6 mm) elastic, with the length equal to the width of the shoe at the instep plus ½" (1.3 cm).

You Will Need

- fabric, for spats and lining
- ¼" (6 mm) foam, for spats interlining
- lightweight fusible interfacing, optional
- elastic, ¼" (6 mm) wide
- hook and loop tape
- plastic nail tips, fingernail polish, glue, for animal spats with claws
- silicone lubricant, for ease in sewing over foam, optional

2 Draw a dotted line perpendicular to lower edge, marking the midpoint. Measure distance from floor over arch of shoe at highest point; add 1" (2.5 cm) for ease, and divide by 2. Mark a point on dotted line this distance from lower edge.

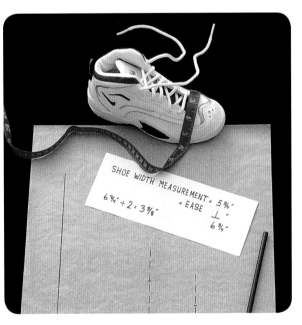

SHOE WIDTH MEASUREMENT = 5 ¾"
6 ¾" ÷ 2 = 3 ⅜"   + EASE
___1___"
6 ¾"

3 Draw a second dotted line, halfway between the midpoint and toe. Measure distance from floor over widest part of shoe at base of toes; add 1" (2.5 cm) for ease, and divide by 2. Mark a point on second dotted line this distance from lower edge. Mark a point 1" (2.5 cm) above toe end of lower edge.

(Continued)

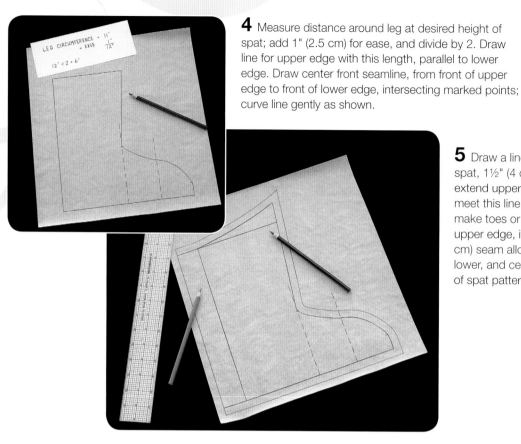

4 Measure distance around leg at desired height of spat; add 1" (2.5 cm) for ease, and divide by 2. Draw line for upper edge with this length, parallel to lower edge. Draw center front seamline, from front of upper edge to front of lower edge, intersecting marked points; curve line gently as shown.

5 Draw a line parallel to back of spat, 1½" (4 cm) from existing line; extend upper and lower edges to meet this line. Shape lower edge to make toes or claws, if desired. Shape upper edge, if desired. Add ½" (1.3 cm) seam allowance around upper, lower, and center front edges of spat pattern. Cut out pattern.

How to Sew Spats

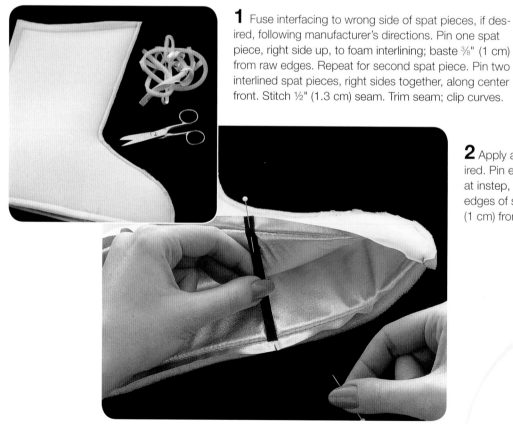

1 Fuse interfacing to wrong side of spat pieces, if desired, following manufacturer's directions. Pin one spat piece, right side up, to foam interlining; baste ⅜" (1 cm) from raw edges. Repeat for second spat piece. Pin two interlined spat pieces, right sides together, along center front. Stitch ½" (1.3 cm) seam. Trim seam; clip curves.

2 Apply appliqués (page 28), if desired. Pin elastic to right side of spat at instep, aligning ends of elastic to edges of spat. Stitch securely, ⅜" (1 cm) from edges.

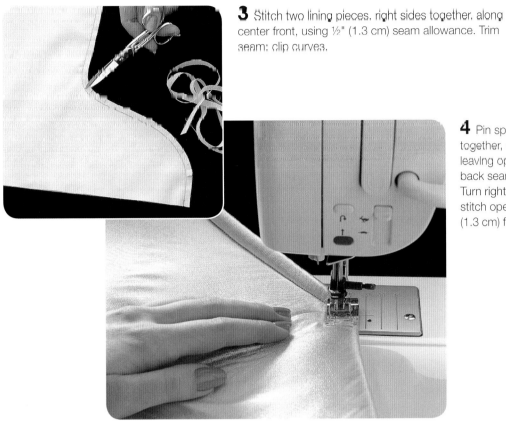

3 Stitch two lining pieces, right sides together, along center front, using ½" (1.3 cm) seam allowance. Trim seam; clip curves.

4 Pin spat to lining, right sides together, stitch ½" (1.3 cm) seam, leaving opening along one center back seam for turning. Trim seam. Turn right side out; press lightly. Slip-stitch opening closed. Topstitch ½" (1.3 cm) from upper and lower edges.

5 Pin hook side of hook and loop tape to wrong side of spat, ⅛" (3 mm) from one center back edge. Pin loop side of tape to right side of spat center back, ⅛" (3 mm) from opposite edge. Stitch around outer edges of tapes.

6 Repeat steps 1 to 5 for second spat, lapping the closure in opposite direction. Stitch any design lines on spats as desired. Add any surface embellishments.

WANDS AND SCEPTERS

Props are an effective addition to any costume. Just as every witch needs a broom, every wizard, magician, or fairy needs a wand and every king or queen needs a scepter. Wands and scepters are easily made from wooden dowels topped with padded fabric stars and glitzy streamers or with Styrofoam balls and small finials. A little paint and some sparkling trims add a magical touch. Hologram or glow-in-the-dark stickers are effective accents for magician and wizard wands. Celestial stickers are often available at science museums, children's toy stores, or party supply stores. Plastic gemstones to decorate a royal scepter can be purchased at craft and fabric stores.

How to Make a Star Wand

1 Cut two pieces of fabric and one piece of foam, larger than desired finished size of star. Apply fusible interfacing to wrong sides of fabric, following manufacturer's directions.

2 Draw or trace a star shape in desired size onto interfaced side of one fabric piece. Layer the fabric pieces, right sides together, over the foam, with star outline on top; pin. Stitch around star, leaving about 3" (7.5 cm) opening on one side for turning.

(Continued)

You Will Need

All Styles:
- craft acrylic paint and paintbrush
- hot glue gun and glue sticks

Star Wand:
- fabric; lightweight fusible interfacing
- ¼" (6 mm) foam, for interlining
- metallic trim, optional
- ⅜" (1 cm) wooden dowel, about 18" (4.5 cm) long
- decorative trims, such as beads, ribbons, and decorative cords

Magician or Wizard Wand:
- dense Styrofoam ball, about 2½" to 3" (6.5 to 7.5 cm) in diameter
- ⅜" (1 cm) wooden dowel, about 18" (45.5 cm) long
- stickers

Royal Scepter:
- ½" (1.3 cm) wooden dowel, 36" (91.5 cm) long
- dense Styrofoam ball, 4" to 6" (10 to 15 cm) in diameter
- macramé bead, doll pin stand, finial, available at craft stores
- assorted plastic gemstones; glue

3 Trim fabric and foam close to stitching. Trim points; clip corners. Turn star right side out; press. Slipstitch opening closed. Topstitch around outer edges. Hand-stitch metallic trim to front of star over stitching line, if desired.

4 Cut trims into desired lengths. Bundle trims, and tie together at center; secure to back of star. Paint dowel handle; allow to dry. Secure handle over trims on back of star, using hot glue.

How to Make a Magician or Wizard Wand

1 Sand Styrofoam ball lightly with sandpaper; wipe with damp rag to remove any powder residue. Poke hole large enough to fit dowel; insert dowel into ball about 1½" (4 cm), securing with hot glue.

2 Apply acrylic paint to ball and dowel; allow to dry. Apply stickers as desired. Embellish the handle, if desired.

Glow-in-the-dark stickers and trims create an aura of mystery.

How to Make a Royal Scepter

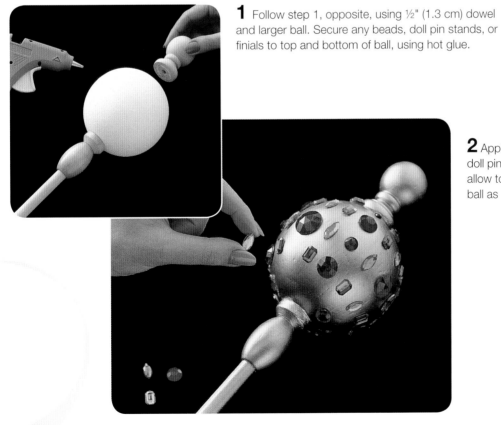

1 Follow step 1, opposite, using ½" (1.3 cm) dowel and larger ball. Secure any beads, doll pin stands, or finials to top and bottom of ball, using hot glue.

2 Apply acrylic paint to ball, bead, doll pin stand, finial, and dowel; allow to dry. Secure gemstones to ball as desired, using hot glue.

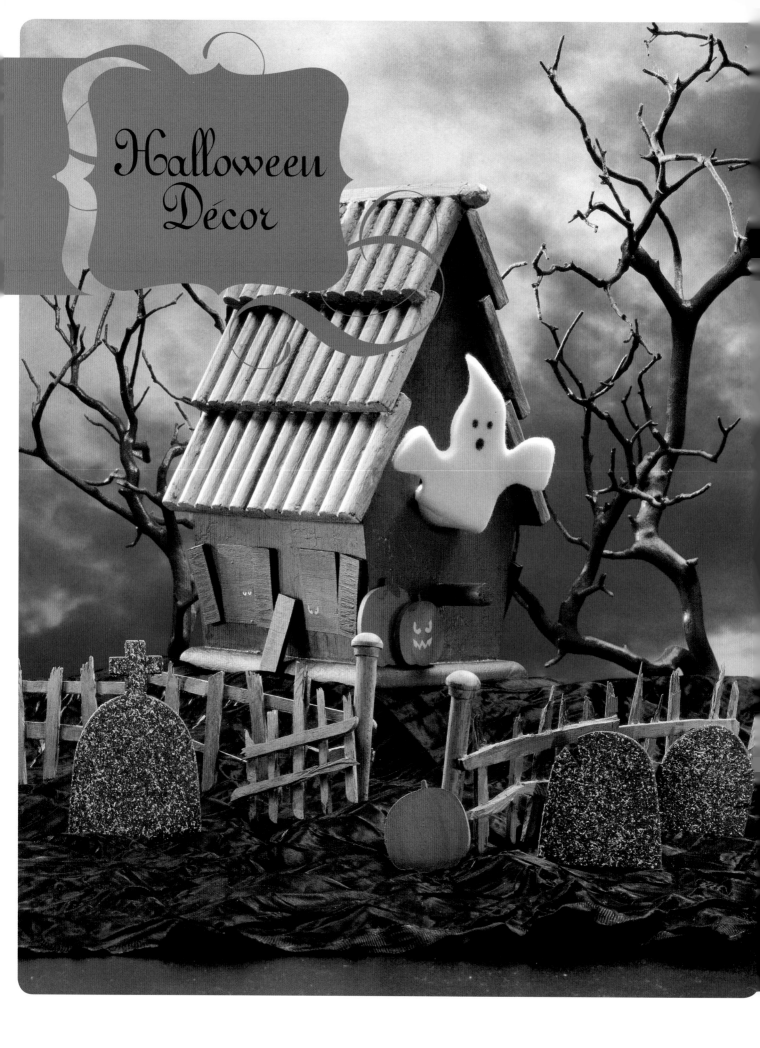

122 Outdoor Greetings

124 Pumpkin Decorating

130 Ghostly Trick-or-Treater

134 Welcome Witch

138 Scarecrow

142 Lighted Swag

144 Stenciled Rugs

146 Haunt the House

148 Harvest Wreath

152 Halloween Swag

156 Tripod Centerpiece

160 Bewitching Shelf

162 Black-tie Skeleton

166 Spiderweb Mobile

172 Scarecrow Wall Hanging

178 Picture Frames

182 Haunted Birdhouses

186 Wooden Shelf Sitters

190 Throw a Party

192 Harlequin Table Runner

196 Pumpkin Table Linens

202 Painted Glass Servers

206 Treat Bag Invitations

210 Foam Treat Cups

214 Placemats

216 Wired Felt Place Cards

218 Buffet Ideas

220 Piñatas

226 Mummy Hands

Outdoor Greetings

PUMPKIN DECORATING

A carved jack-o'-lantern is the original Halloween luminary. Transforming pumpkins and squashes into glowing globes with friendly smiles or frightful sneers is the cornerstone activity for Halloween merrymaking. With the use of a few simple tools, elaborate expressions and spooky silhouettes are easily carved or sculpted by novice and artist alike. Inexpensive carving kits that include tiny saws, a poker for marking the pattern, and a miniature drill make pumpkin carving as easy as connecting the dots.

Greet Halloween night visitors with a glowing array of carved and sculpted pumpkins and squashes. Or paint pumpkins with spirited designs, for lasting enjoyment during daylight hours.

Because of the sharp blades, carving and sculpting pumpkins requires careful adult participation, though older children can carve intricate designs safely. Designs can also be sculpted into the surface of pumpkins and squashes using tools intended for other purposes: linoleum cutters cut fine lines; gouges and chisels cut deeper into the pulp.

Use the patterns on page 231, enlarging them as necessary. Or develop your own designs from simple line drawings. If you intend to carve, cutting completely through the pumpkin shell, be sure any area you want to silhouette will remain connected to the intact shell. Draw patterns for sculpting, shading areas as you want them to appear. Lighter areas are sculpted deeper, and dark areas are left uncut. Incorporate both techniques into the same design, if you prefer.

Painted pumpkins can be used indoors as well as outside. Because the shells are uncut, they can be decorated long before Halloween and still look fresh for Thanksgiving. Painting on pumpkins is also a safer activity for younger children. Apply acrylic craft paints, using paintbrushes, foam applicators, or shapes cut from cellulose sponges.

Select firm pumpkins and squashes with sturdy stems, an indication that the pumpkins will last longer. Wash them thoroughly with a weak bleach solution. Store the pumpkins at least 1" (2.5 cm) apart in a cool, dry, well-ventilated area. Do not allow them to freeze. Once cut, pumpkins may dry out and the edges will shrivel. For best results, carve or sculpt pumpkins less than 24 hours before use. Cover the openings and the design with plastic and keep them cold. If they will be displayed for an extended time, rub petroleum jelly on the exposed pulp.

Whether carving, sculpting, or painting a pumpkin, never set a pumpkin or candle directly on furniture. Never leave a candle unattended indoors. Place lit pumpkins where they won't tip or fall, and keep them out of the walkway.

You Will Need

- pumpkin or squash
- newspaper
- paper, pencil, scissors, tape

For Carving and Sculpting:
- small handsaw, 6" (15 cm) blade with narrow tip, for carving lid and large open areas
- ice cream scoop or sturdy spoon
- carving tools, such as awl, linoleum cutters, gouges, chisels, or melon ball tool
- candle and candle holder, size appropriate for pumpkin size

For Painting:
- graphite paper
- acrylic paints
- artist's brushes; foam applicators, cellulose sponges
- permanent markers, optional
- aerosol clear acrylic sealer

How to Carve a Pumpkin

1 Cut an opening in the top or bottom of the pumpkin large enough for removing seeds and pulp. If cutting a top lid, angle tool inward, so lid will not fall into shell. If cutting bottom opening, cut straight into pumpkin. Cover work surface with newspaper. Clean out seeds and pulp, using ice cream scoop or spoon. Scrape shell wall to consistent 1" (2.5 cm) thickness.

(Continued)

2 Trace or draw a pattern on paper. Tape pattern to pumpkin; slash and lap pattern as necessary to fit pumpkin smoothly, without distorting design details. Poke small holes every ⅛" (3 mm) along all design lines, using pushpin, awl, or poking tool. Remove pattern; set aside. Connect dots in intricate areas with pencil.

3 Gently twist small drill bit to cut any round holes, keeping drill perpendicular to the pumpkin surface. For tiny points of light, push awl or poking tool entirely through the pumpkin shell.

4 Carve small details first, working from center of design outward. Hold saw perpendicular to surface; saw gently, dot to dot. Remove and reinsert blade to turn corners. Keep free hand away from saw; avoid pressing on carved areas. Saw large pieces into smaller pieces; push them out with your fingers. Trim excess pulp around the openings, cutting at slight angle.

How to Sculpt a Pumpkin or Squash

1 Follow steps 1 and 2 on pages 125–126. Carve simple lines first, using linoleum cutter, gouge, or chisel. Rotate pumpkin, always cutting away from body; stabilize pumpkin from behind cutting tool, to avoid cutting hand.

2 Sculpt light and medium areas of design, cutting away desired amount of pulp. The deeper the cuts, the more light will shine through. To sculpt large area, cut away pulp, using melon ball tool.

How to Light a Carved or Sculpted Pumpkin

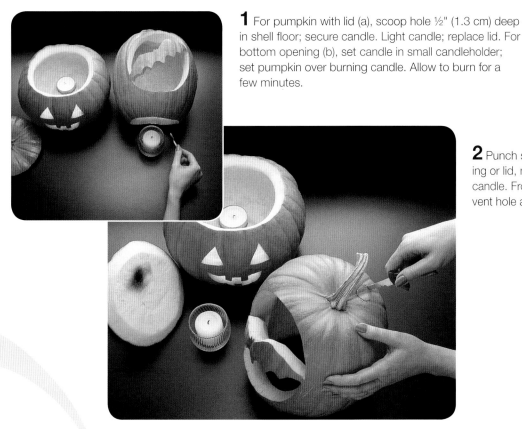

1 For pumpkin with lid (a), scoop hole ½" (1.3 cm) deep in shell floor; secure candle. Light candle; replace lid. For bottom opening (b), set candle in small candleholder; set pumpkin over burning candle. Allow to burn for a few minutes.

2 Punch small hole through shell ceiling or lid, marking area darkened by candle. From outside, cut 1" (2.5 cm) vent hole around the mark.

Tips for Painting on Pumpkins and Squashes

Transfer intricate designs, using graphite paper. Draw simple designs freehand, using pencil or felt-tip pen.

Add bold design lines, using permanent markers.

Apply acrylic paint, using artist's brushes or small foam applicators. Paint background colors first. Allow the paint to dry thoroughly before applying foreground colors. Apply two or three coats as necessary.

Spray dry designs with aerosol clear acrylic sealer.

Cut Halloween shapes from cellulose sponges. Coat surface of sponge with paint; roll across pumpkin surface for even coverage.

More Ideas for Decorating Pumpkins and Squashes

Stack carved or painted pumpkins or squashes to create Halloween creatures. Join them with sturdy toothpicks or wood skewers.

Incorporate odd shapes or blemishes into your design, rather than hide them. Lay pumpkin on its side and use the stem for a nose. Change bumps and nodes into warts or beauty marks.

GHOSTLY TRICK-OR-TREATER

Surprise trick-or-treaters who come knocking at your door with this little guy to greet them. He looks so real that you may even try to load his trick-or-treat basket when you're filling all the others!

Under his felt ghost costume is a simple support system of wooden dowels, wire, and Styrofoam balls. Use jeans and shoes that a child has outgrown for a touch of reality; shop at a local thrift store if you don't have anything close at hand. Top off the little character with a child's baseball cap. Then sit back and listen to others say hello to him before they ring your doorbell. When you trick them, you have to treat them, too!

How to Make a Ghostly Trick-or-Treater

1 Cut 6" (15 cm) length of wire; fold into tight "U" shape. Poke ends through small Styrofoam ball and into large Styrofoam ball, for head.

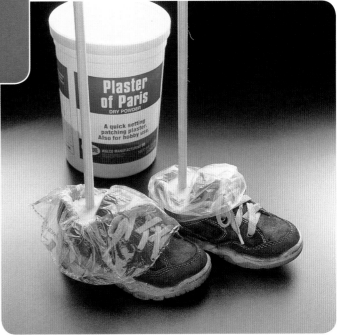

You Will Need

- 18-gauge wire; wire cutter
- two Styrofoam balls; 1" (2.5 cm), for nose; 6" (15 cm), for head
- two ⅜" (1 cm) dowels; 36" (91.5 cm) long
- one pair used children's shoes, size 7 to 9½
- two plastic bags to fit inside shoes
- plaster of Paris and disposable container for mixing
- one pair used children's jeans, size 3 to 5
- newspaper
- hot glue gun
- 1¾ yd. (1.6 m) white felt, 72" (183 cm) wide
- straightedge, pencil, scissors
- black fabric scrap, for eyes
- paper-backed fusible web and iron
- purchased trick-or-treat basket
- child's cap

2 Line shoes with plastic bags. Prepare plaster of Paris, following manufacturer's directions. Pour plaster into bags, filling shoes. Set aside to harden; insert dowels into shoes and prop upright just before plaster is fully set. Allow to dry thoroughly.

(Continued)

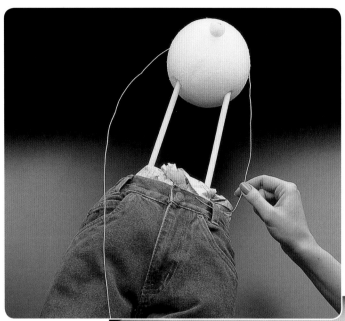

3 Tuck plastic bags into shoes. Slip jeans legs over dowels; stuff jeans with newspaper for body shape. Push both dowels into head so nose is positioned properly; secure with hot glue. Push wire through head, from side to side; secure one end to jeans belt loop.

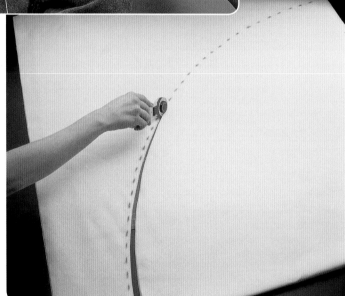

4 Fold felt in half lengthwise, then crosswise. Using straightedge and pencil, mark an arc on felt, 30" (76 cm) from folded center. Cut on the marked line through all layers. Drape unfolded felt over head so lower edge is even.

5 Draw two ovals on paper side of fusible web. Bond to black fabric, following manufacturer's directions. Cut out ovals; pin to felt at eye level. Remove felt; fuse ovals in place.

6 Replace felt over head. Cut 3" (7.5 cm) horizontal slit in felt, at hip level, on side where wire is unsecured. Bring wire through slit; wrap around purchased trick-or-treat basket.

WELCOME WITCH

Beware of Esmerelda. Flying just above the ground, she greets your Halloween visitors. Place her along the walkway or near the front door. You can create other welcoming figures, drawing your own patterns or enlarging and tracing favorite Halloween shapes.

Purchase an exterior plywood with a weather-resistant glue because regular plywood may split and warp when wet, even if it is painted and sealed; find ¼" (6 mm) exterior plywood at wood hobby stores or ⅜" (1 cm) at lumberyards. Buy regular plywood if you plan to stand her on your porch or even inside.

Make simple stakes from two clothes hangers and push them easily into the ground to keep Esmerelda from falling in mid-flight.

How to Make a Welcome Witch

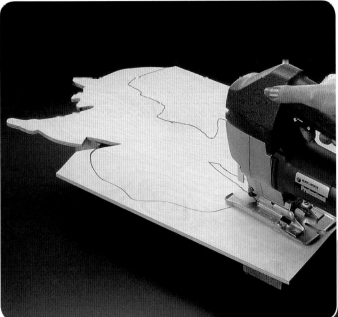

1 Enlarge the pattern (page 236); cut out. Trace onto plywood. Cut along marked lines, using saw. Sand rough edges.

You Will Need

- ¼" or ⅜" (6 mm or 1 cm) plywood, about 12" × 24" (30.5 × 61 cm)
- graphite paper
- masking tape
- coping saw or jigsaw
- medium-grit sandpaper
- ⅜" (1 cm) dowel, 36" (91.5 cm) long
- wood glue
- 9½" × 9½" × ¾" (24.1 × 24.1 × 2 cm) board, for base
- drill; ¹⁄₁₆", ⅛", and ⅜" drill bits
- 28-gauge wire and wire cutter
- sanding sealer
- acrylic paint, colors as desired
- polyurethane
- two wire clothes hangers

2 Mark dowel 2" (5 cm) from one end. Round end slightly; flatten one side above mark, using sandpaper.

(Continued)

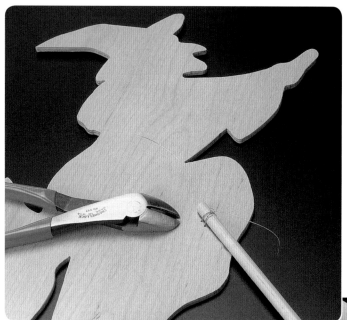

3 Glue flat side of dowel to back of cut shape. Drill two holes on each side of dowel, using ¹⁄₁₆" drill bit; space holes ¼" (6 mm) apart. Pass wire through each hole two or three times, pulling snug. Twist ends together; trim ends.

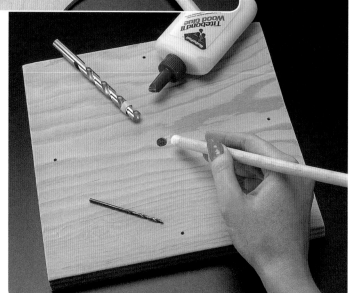

4 Wrap tape around ⅜ drill bit with edge of tape ⅝" (1.5 cm) from tip. Drill hole at center of base, stopping when edge of tape meets surface of wood. To stake base in lawn, drill hole through base, ¾" (2 cm) from each side center, using ⅛" drill bit. Sand rough edges. Glue dowel in center hole of board.

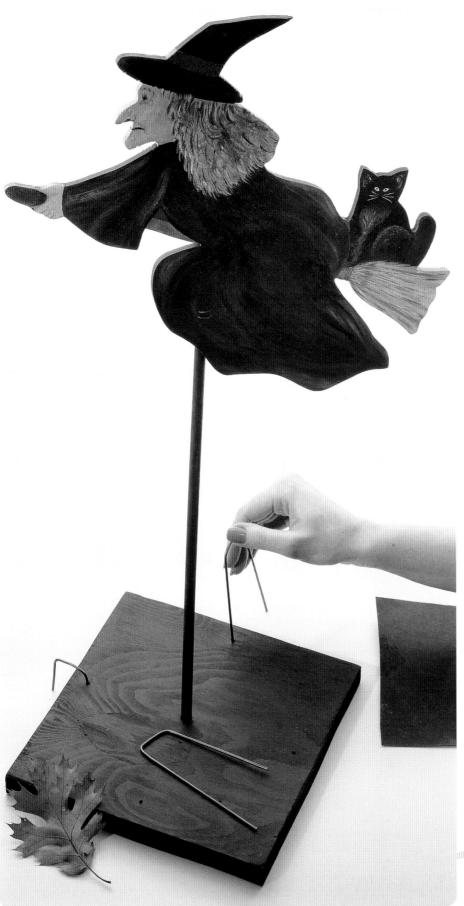

5 Apply sanding sealer to witch, dowel, and base. Paint as desired; allow to dry. Apply polyurethane; allow to dry. Form two stakes from each hanger, if desired. Cut wire 5" (12.5 cm) from each lower corner, bend wire 1" (2.5 cm) beyond corners, and trim second side to 5" (12.5 cm). Insert stakes through base holes and into ground.

SCARECROW

Stand this proud scarecrow to guard your home and greet your friendly visitors. Dress him in cast-off clothing and stuff him with raffia. Collect pumpkins and hay bales at his feet and set a raven on his shoulder to show the world that he, too, is a friendly guy.

Find suitable clothing as close as a child's closet or find something inexpensive at a thrift shop. Look for pants that have a snap inseam for convenience, or cut a small hole just behind the crotch seams. Select from a wide variety of hat styles and embellishments to make your scarecrow unique.

How to Make a Scarecrow

1 Drill hole through base center, using ½" drill bit. Sand rough edges. Glue dowel into base; allow to dry. Paint or stain as desired; dry. Apply two coats of sealer, following manufacturer's directions. Predrill hole for screw eye on front of dowel, 2" (5 cm) from top, using ³⁄₃₂" drill bit; insert screw eye. Drop overalls or jeans onto dowel through inseam crotch.

2 Cut 9" (23 cm) length of 18-gauge wire. Form 8 oz. (250 g) raffia into bundle. Wrap wire around center; pull tight, and twist wires once or twice, leaving excess length.

(Continued)

You Will Need

- 9½" × 9½" × ¾" (24.3 × 24.3 × 2 cm) board, for base
- saw, sandpaper
- drill, ½" and ³⁄₃₂" drill bits
- ½" × 36" (1.3 × 91.5 cm) wood dowel
- wood glue
- sealer, such as water-based polyurethane
- paint or stain, for stand
- #212 screw eye
- child's bib overalls, size 4, or jeans and four large safety pins
- 24-oz. (750 g) packages raffia
- 18-gauge wire
- plastic hanger
- child's flannel shirt, size 4, used
- scissors
- ⅝ yd. (0.6 m) burlap
- hot glue gun
- 6" (15 cm) Styrofoam ball
- twine
- paints, for face
- hat
- embellishments as desired: raven, bandanna, fall flowers, or miniature corncobs

3 Wire hanger, upside down, to back of dowel at screw eye. Wire raffia bundle to hanger hook; wire hook to dowel, using excess wire of raffia bundle. Reach into each leg and pull raffia through; allow raffia to puddle on base.

4 Repeat step 2 to make second raffia bundle; separate wire tails. Assemble third raffia bundle; lay over second bundle. Wrap and twist wires to secure.

5 Wire double raffia bundle to front of dowel at screw eye; separate bundles. Wire third raffia bundle loosely to hanger ends.

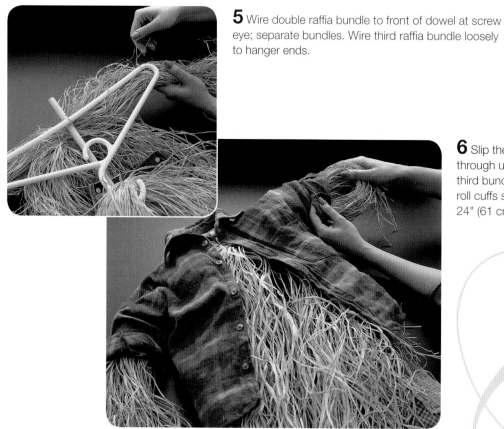

6 Slip the shirt over hanger. Reach through unbuttoned sleeves and pull third bundle out. Scrunch sleeves or roll cuffs so sleeve ends are about 24" (61 cm) apart.

7 Button shirt, and tuck into pants with second bundle. Add more raffia to fatten waist area, if desired. Hook shoulder straps to bib, or pin shirt inside jeans. Trim raffia at hands to about 3" (7.5 cm). Trim feet, if desired.

8 Push Styrofoam ball onto dowel end until it hits the screw eye. Remove ball. Apply glue to hole and dowel; reposition ball on dowel, for head.

9 Fold the burlap in half lengthwise, then crosswise; pin. Mark an arc on burlap, measuring 11" (28 cm) from folded center. Cut on marked line through all layers. Trim away one quarter of the circle.

10 Center burlap over head; lap at back, and tie at neck with twine and raffia. Ravel burlap, if desired. Add facial details, using acrylic paints. Tie bandanna around neck, hiding twine, if desired. Add other embellishments as desired.

LIGHTED SWAG

Colorful images allow visitors to enjoy this sway before the sun goes down, but it's even more fun in the dark! Children of all ages will enjoy making the simple decorations that appear in the black night behind small lights.

Purchase lightweight foam sheets, available in many colors, at craft stores, and cut delightful or frightful shapes, using ordinary scissors. Use cookie cutters for inspiration, or develop your own designs, incorporating a miniature light bulb. Try a jack-o'-lantern with an extra-bright nose or a fire-breathing dragon.

Avoid dark foam colors for the primary shape, since they will melt into the blackness beyond; reserve dark colors for surface embellishments. Just in case the weather turns wet and gloomy, secure design layers with a low-temperature glue gun or a waterproof glue.

How to Make a Lighted Swag

1 Cut simple Halloween shapes from craft foam, using cookie cutters for patterns or drawing designs as desired. Cut two ¼" (6 mm) crossed slits in each shape at desired location for light, using mat knife.

2 Embellish shapes as desired; attach foam detail shapes, using glue for added dimension, or draw design lines, using markers.

You Will Need

- foam sheets, assorted colors
- cookie cutters, optional
- pencil
- scissors with plain or decorative-edge blades
- low-temperature glue gun or waterproof glue
- mat knife
- permanent markers, optional
- weatherproof miniature lights
- grapevine or honeysuckle swag

3 Entwine string of lights throughout swag, spacing lights evenly and pointing lights toward front of swag. Push crossed slits over the light and bulb housing. Pull foam back to edge of housing and bulb, turning slit edges back.

STENCILED RUGS

This easy and inexpensive stenciled rug, made from a carpet sample, greets your Halloween visitors. An easy shake will clean it, and it stands up to a vacuum or a damp sponge, too.

Choose a carpet sample with a short, dense pile. Enlarge designs from other projects or create your own. Keep designs simple; the texture of the carpet is too coarse for fine details.

Cut a stencil of self-adhesive vinyl. Draw designs freehand, or trace a design using graphite paper or by holding it up to a light source. The stencil must adhere well to the carpet; press firmly around the cut edges of the stencil to improve the bond.

Condition the paint with fabric medium, following the manufacturer's directions, or thin two parts paint with one part water so the paint will be absorbed into the pile.

How to Make a Stenciled Rug

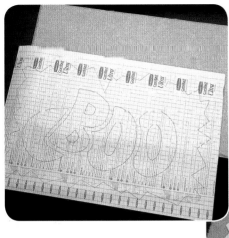

1 Cut self adhesive vinyl to fit carpet sample. Draw or trace design, including outer border, on paper side of vinyl; draw mirror image of any letters or numbers.

2 Cut away areas to be stenciled, using mat knife or scissors. Remove paper backing from stencil carefully; press firmly onto carpet.

3 Apply conditioned or thinned paint to exposed carpet, using stencil brush or sponge applicator. Use an up-and-down motion, working paint into the fibers. Allow to dry.

You Will Need

- carpet sample with bound edges
- self-adhesive vinyl, such as Con-Tact
- graphite paper, optional
- mat knife and cutting surface
- acrylic paints
- fabric medium, optional
- firm stencil brush or sponge applicator
- hair dryer
- stiff brush
- aerosol clear acrylic sealer, optional

4 Remove stencil. Apply additional stencils, if desired. Allow to dry. Heat-set paint with hair dryer. Use stiff brush to soften painted areas. Apply sealer, if desired.

Haunt the House

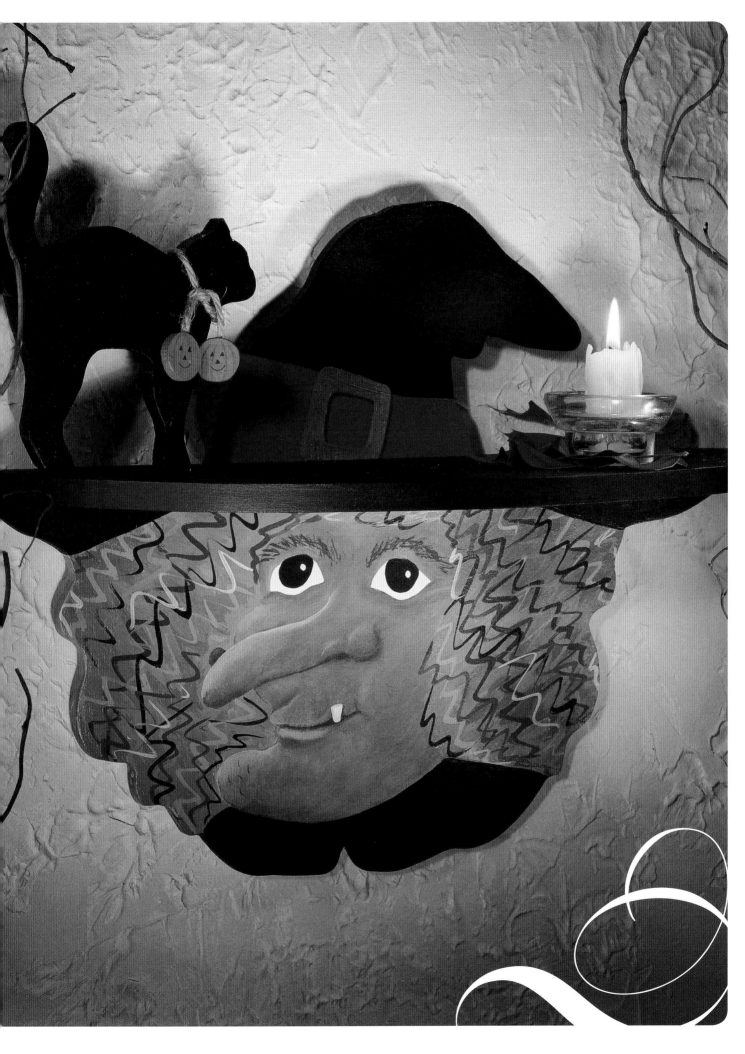

HARVEST WREATH

This beautiful grapevine wreath is the perfect accent for a wall or door as it brings the colors of the season inside. By removing the Halloween cookie cutters, you can extend the life of the wreath into the Thanksgiving harvest season.

Secure larger items to the wreath with floral wire; secure smaller items with hot glue. Flexible wire, available on a paddle, is cut to the desired length; stem wire is stiffer and is packaged in 18" (46 cm) lengths. When covered with brown floral tape, wires blend with the smaller branches of the grapevine. The use of floral spray paints is optional; they may be used to deepen natural tones, to introduce gold highlights, or to provide a rich sheen.

How to Make a Harvest Wreath

1 Wrap taped floral wire around corn, between ears and husk; secure corn to wreath, twisting wire ends.

You Will Need

- 18" (46 cm) grapevine wreath
- floral wire, wire cutter, wired wooden floral picks, brown floral tape
- Indian corn ears with husks, assorted sizes
- pinecones; acorns, assorted sizes
- miniature pumpkins, fresh or artificial
- lotus pods
- copper Halloween cookie cutters
- hot glue gun

2 Wrap wire around bottom layers of larger pinecones, twisting to secure. Use wire or glue to attach group of medium and large cones near each ear of corn. Push wire through fresh pumpkins or push wired pick into artificial pumpkins. Wrap wire around wreath near lowest ear of corn; twist to secure.

(Continued)

3 Glue lotus pods behind cones; add husks as desired. Use small cones and acorns to hide corn wires and enhance groups of pods and cones.

4 Attach cookie cutters to floral picks; wire to wreath behind pinecones. Twist taped wire to form loop; wrap ends around top of wreath for hanger.

More Wreath Ideas

Black-tie skeleton (page 162) nestles comfortably in the curve of the wreath. Secure the skeleton, using fine wire or monofilament line.

Substitute wired felt forms (page 217) or painted cardboard shapes for the cookie cutters.

Substitute colorful fall leaves for the locust pods and cones. Replace the Indian corn with fall florals, such as mums or sunflowers.

HALLOWEEN SWAG

Birds, bats, and spiders find an inviting perch in this eerie Halloween swag. The wild, mysterious look of this piece is achieved in the selection of its elements. Look for dried naturals in dark, rich colors, and complement them with lighter tones. Artemisia, for example, is a silvery green, though you may also find it dyed other colors. Curly ting-ting is a thin, spiraling branch available in a variety of colors. Black Beard wheat offers a dramatic accent, both in shape and color.

Use fresh gourds and pumpkins if you intend to keep the swag for only a short time. Once they are pierced with wire, they will begin to disintegrate. Substitute dried or artificial items to extend the life of the swag.

How to Make a Halloween Swag

1 Form swag with twigs, honeysuckle vine, and grapevine pieces; bind with taped wire about one-third of the distance from each end. Twist taped wire to form loop for hanging; secure one loop behind each binding wire.

2 Cut five foam pieces ½" (1.3 cm) thick, and glue to central length of swag. Glue moss to swag, covering the foam.

(Continued)

You Will Need

- twigs, honeysuckle vine, and grapevine pieces, 36" to 40" (91.5 to 102 cm) long
- floral wire, wire cutter, brown floral tape
- floral foam for dried arranging; serrated knife
- gray moss
- hot glue gun
- dried naturals, including artemisia, Sweet Annie, Black Beard wheat, step grass, and curly ting-ting
- small gourds, miniature pumpkins
- floral picks, drill and small drill bit, optional
- miniature ears red popcorn
- old nylon hose, gray; scissors
- plastic spiders, heavy invisible thread
- blackbird, 2" to 3" (5 to 7.5 cm) long, on pick
- wired felt bats (page 216) or plastic clip-on bats

3 Apply glue to ends of dried naturals; insert into foam from left and right of center. Add curly ting-ting.

4 Rub gold wax-based paint onto gourds or pumpkins, if desired. Push wire through fresh gourds. Insert wire ends through foam and around several vine pieces; twist ends, and trim. Or insert a pick well into drilled hole of dried gourd. Apply glue to both ends of pick and insert into foam as vertically as possible.

5 Shred gray nylon hose with scissors and fingernails. Drape, twist, and stretch hose over and around vines and moss to imitate cobwebs.

6 Rub gold wax-based paint onto corn ear kernels and husks as desired. Wrap taped wire around corn, between ears and husks. Secure corn to swag.

7 Glue spiders to the cobweb; use invisible thread to dangle the spiders, if desired. Push blackbird into the foam. Attach bats to ting-ting.

TRIPOD CENTERPIECE

This haunting arrangement seems to have come from the distant corner of a crumbling mansion. Long forgotten, the crows and spiders have made it their home, and even a couple of bats find it welcoming.

The tripod consists of three sturdy branches about 25" (63.5 cm) long and about ½" (1.3 cm) in diameter at their thickest. Look for branches with interesting twists and nubby knots. Three similar sticks are used to brace the tripod form.

A small handleless basket or bird's nest holds the fall harvest. Fresh gourds and pumpkins may be used for a week or two, but select dried or artificial varieties if you plan to keep the arrangement for a long time. The eerie cobwebs are actually shredded nylon hose!

How to Make a Tripod Centerpiece

1 Wrap branches together about mid-length, using taped wire. Spread thicker ends to form tripod. Attach basket rim to each branch with taped wire; twist and trim excess wire length.

2 Brace tripod with three small sticks; wire to branches just below the basket. Glue small weights inside basket to stabilize, if desired.

(Continued)

You Will Need

- three branches and three small sticks
- floral wire, wire cutter, brown floral tape
- shallow basket or bird's nest, 5" to 6" (12.5 to 15 cm) in diameter
- small weights, optional
- floral foam for dried arranging; serrated knife
- green moss
- floral pins
- small gourds or miniature pumpkins
- gold wax-based paint, optional
- floral picks, drill and small drill bit, optional
- pods
- black crow, about 4" (10 cm) long
- old nylon hose, gray; scissors
- small plastic spiders
- wired felt bats (page 216)
- hot glue gun

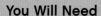

3 Cut foam, using knife, so it fits basket snugly and sits ½" (1.3 cm) below rim. Glue foam into basket. Secure moss over foam with floral pins. Glue moss pieces over each wired joint.

4 Rub gold wax-based paint onto two or three gourds, if desired. Attach all gourds and pumpkins to basket, using wire, floral picks, or hot glue. Push pods into foam near outer edge of basket.

5 Shred two or three pieces of nylon hose, using scissors or fingernails. Drape, twist, and stretch hose over branches to resemble cobwebs.

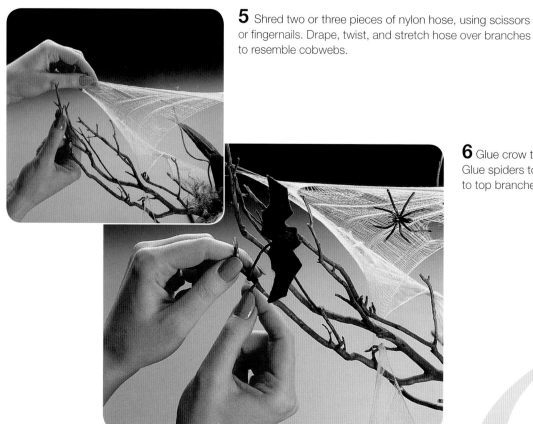

6 Glue crow to moss at upper joint. Glue spiders to cobwebs; attach bats to top branches.

More Ideas for Tripods and Swags

Substitute a plastic witch's cauldron for the tripod basket. Use small straw brooms, reinforced with dowels, for the three legs of the tripod; bind them with raffia or twine. Build a fire of small branches below the cauldron, with red foil to imitate the flames. Attach a glittering moon to an upper limb and a giant bat or raven to guard the brew.

Add miniature brooms to the swag. Wind a string of lights covered with witch and moon foam shapes through the swag. Substitute leaves for gourds. Wire the swag to a straight branch for support.

Substitute a carved pumpkin or a foam jack-o'-lantern for the basket. Perch a beanbag pumpkin overhead and arrange little wired felt ghosts to dance among the branches.

Cut the top from a Styrofoam pumpkin, using a serrated knife. Paint the inside and rim to match outside.

BEWITCHING SHELF

This beguiling witch with her haunting smile will be a whimsical addition to any room.
There's a touch of good witchcraft about her—the hat brim is also a shelf. It's the perfect
place for an extra candle, a friendly gourd, or a favorite black cat. When this shelf hangs on
the wall, it's easy to see who's the fairest of them all!

How to Make a Witch Shelf

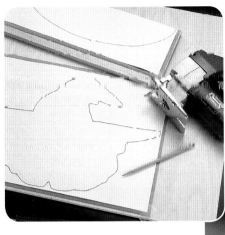

1 Enlarge witch's face pattern (page 237). Draw pattern for brim shelf 5" (12.5 cm) deep at center, with length equal to enlarged pattern brim; curve front brim edge toward sides. Tape patterns over graphite paper on wood; trace outlines and design lines. Cut out, using jigsaw.

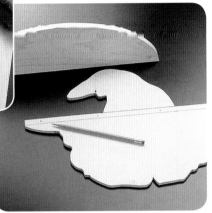

2 Stand the brim back on wrong side of face; align brim's upper side with face's straight edge. Mark each side of brim; set brim aside. Mark placement for four evenly spaced pilot holes halfway between brim lines; mark outer holes about 1" (2.5 cm) from ends.

3 Secure brim in clamp so straight edge is at top. Place right side of face on brim; align straight edge with brim top. Drill holes with countersink bit at each mark.

You Will Need

- ¼" (6 mm) finish-grade plywood, for face
- ½" × 6" (1.3 × 15 cm) poplar board, at least 18" (46 cm) long, for hat brim
- graphite paper
- jigsaw, clamp
- drill; ⅛" combination drill and counter-sink bit
- wood glue
- four #8 × 1⅝" (4 cm) coarse-thread drywall screws
- 180-grit sandpaper
- acrylic paints in desired colors
- two sawtooth hangers

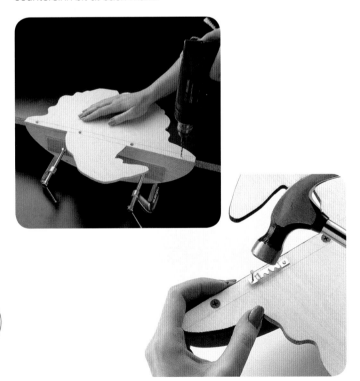

4 Apply glue lightly to both pieces of wood. Realign, and secure with screws. Sand rough edges. Paint as desired. Attach sawtooth hangers near straight edge, through back and into shelf.

BLACK-TIE SKELETON

Haunt your house with the eerie sound of dry bones clickety-clacking in the wind. Hang this black-tie skeleton on your front door where it will clatter every time you greet a friendly monster. Pose him reclining in the curve of a wreath or seated, with legs dangling from a shelf.

Aside from his dowel limbs, all of his parts are made from precut wood pieces and beads, available at craft and hobby stores. Paint Mr. Bones with acrylic paints, following the example here, or leave him unpainted for a natural look.

How to Make a Black-tie Skeleton

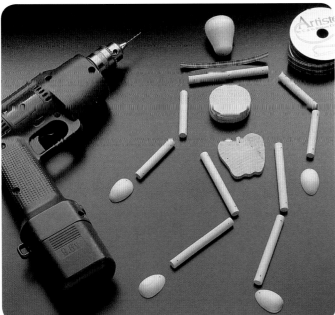

1 Stack oval cutouts; clamp together. Drill hole ½" (1.3 cm) from outer edge of one long side, using ¹⁄₁₆" drill bit. Drill hole ¼" (6 mm) from each end of each dowel piece; drill hole in middle of shoulder piece. Clamp dowel pieces to work surface to be sure all holes are centered and parallel. Drill hole through apple cutout at base of stem, drill hole ¼" (6 mm) from edge at center of each side. Drill hole ¼" (6 mm) from narrow end of two egg shapes for feet; drill hole ¼" (6 mm) from wide end of two egg shapes for hands. Predrill shallow hole in center of narrow end of pear, for screw eye. Repeat at wide end, for hanging skeleton.

2 Sand any rough edges, using 100-grit sandpaper. Paint all pieces as desired. String wooden spools and beads; suspend over shoe box, for ease in painting. Paint skull features; add any other accents as desired. Apply acrylic sealer, if desired.

(Continued)

You Will Need

- ⅜" (1 cm) wood dowel, 36" (91.5 cm) long
- wood pear, 2" (5 cm) high
- one wooden apple cutout, 2¼" (6 cm) high
- four 2" × 1⅝" (5 × 4 cm) oval wooden cutouts
- six ½" × ½" (1.3 × 1.3 cm) wooden spools
- four small wooden split robin eggs
- twelve 10 mm round wooden beads
- two screw eyes, size #214
- small saw, 100-grit sandpaper
- craft acrylic paints: white and black or glow-in-the-dark paint
- aerosol clear acrylic sealer, optional
- drill and ¹⁄₁₆" drill bit
- lightweight monofilament fishing line
- black grosgrain ribbon, ¼" (6 mm wide)

Cutting Directions

Cut four 2½" (6.5 cm) dowel pieces for the arms. Cut four 3½" (9 cm) dowel pieces for the legs. Cut one 4" (10 cm) dowel piece for the shoulders.

3 Insert screw eye in narrow end of skull. String skull, neck, shoulders, vertebrae, ribs, and pelvis together to bottom and back up to top; pull line snug, and knot securely.

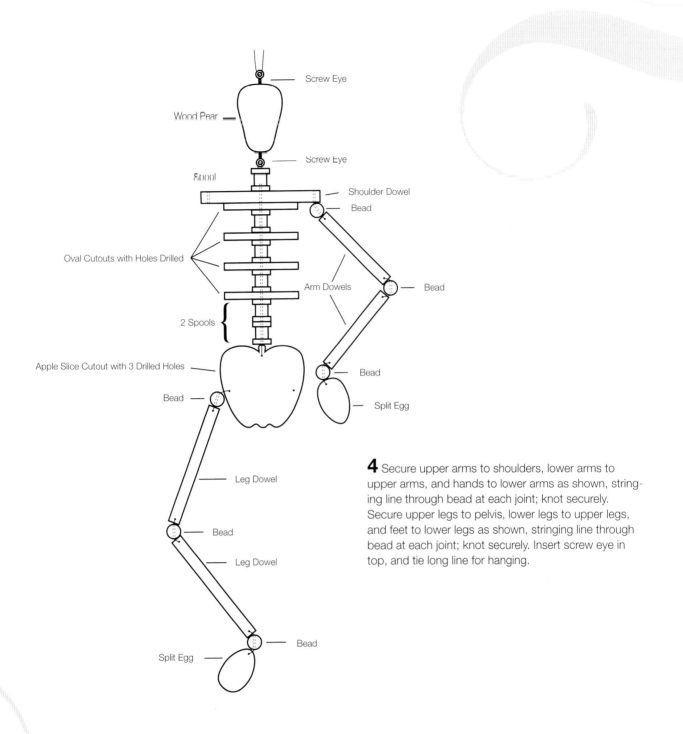

Screw Eye

Wood Pear

Screw Eye

Spool

Shoulder Dowel

Bead

Oval Cutouts with Holes Drilled

Arm Dowels

Bead

2 Spools

Apple Slice Cutout with 3 Drilled Holes

Bead

Split Egg

Bead

Leg Dowel

Bead

Leg Dowel

Bead

Split Egg

4 Secure upper arms to shoulders, lower arms to upper arms, and hands to lower arms as shown, stringing line through bead at each joint; knot securely. Secure upper legs to pelvis, lower legs to upper legs, and feet to lower legs as shown, stringing line through bead at each joint; knot securely. Insert screw eye in top, and tie long line for hanging.

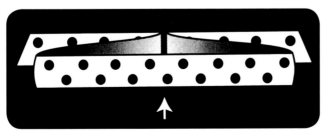

5 Fold 6" (15 cm) piece of black grosgrain ribbon into bow tie as shown; hand-stitch at center. Wrap center tightly with thread; knot on back. Stitch or glue bow tie to front of lower screw eye.

SPIDERWEB MOBILE

This spider has the Halloween spirit! Suspend her fanciful spiderweb in a doorway or from a light fixture where it will delight unsuspecting guests.

Wrap a wooden embroidery hoop with dental floss to form the web. Use various lengths of floss to suspend polymer clay shapes from the web.

Knead polymer clay with your hands for several minutes, until it is pliable enough to form shapes, press into molds, or roll flat for cutting. Clean your hands with a disposable towel-ette before working with another clay color. Use Halloween candy molds or fashion your own little critters. Ease removal of the clay from candy molds with a very light dusting of baby powder.

How to Make a Spiderweb Mobile

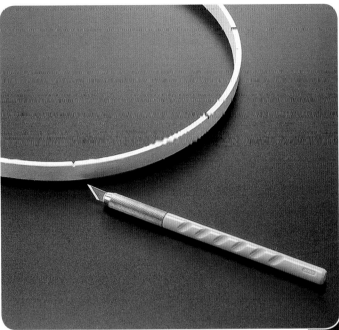

1 Mark eight evenly spaced points about 3⅞" (9.7 cm) apart along top edge of inner hoop. Notch the hoop at each mark, using craft knife.

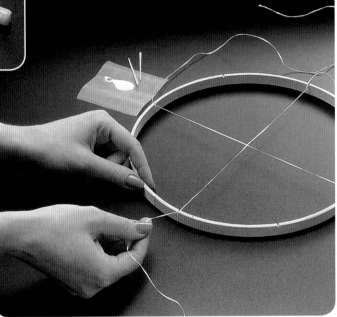

2 Tie dental floss at two opposing marks, leaving 24" (61 cm) tails for hangers. Repeat at two more opposing marks, forming an "X" through the center. Apply dot of craft glue on knots, using toothpick.

(Continued)

You Will Need

- wooden embroidery hoop, 10" (25.5 cm) diameter
- dental floss tape, for web
- mat knife
- craft glue
- small plastic ring
- polymer clay, black and assorted colors
- toothpick, aluminum foil
- disposable towelettes
- baking sheet
- assorted candy molds, baby powder, small soft paintbrush, screw eyes, for 3D shapes
- assorted cookie cutters, large dowel, for flat shapes
- acrylic paints, optional

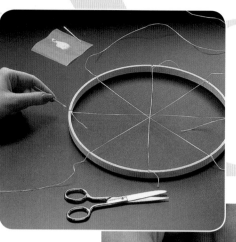

3 Tie floss at remaining opposing marks, forming second "X". Apply dot of glue on each knot; trim excess floss close to knots. Do not trim hanger tails.

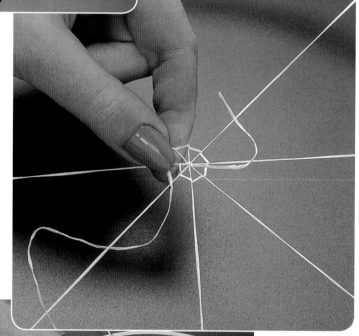

4 Tie floss to center intersection, securing all strands together. Wrap floss around one strand, about ⅜" (1 cm) from center. Continue to wrap floss once around each strand of web in a spiral, holding onto previous wrap to prevent it from slipping.

5 Apply glue to each wrap after completing round of eight wraps. Continue wrapping the floss at each strand; glue wraps after each round.

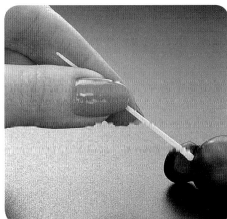

6 Roll two polymer clay balls of ½" and ¼" (1.3 cm and 6 mm) diameter for the spider body. Flatten larger ball slightly on one side and attach smaller ball as shown. Smooth two balls together, using toothpick. Roll small amount of clay into ⅜" (1 cm) long rod, pointing ends; attach to underside of the head, for pincers.

7 Roll clay into four thin rods, about 2¾" (7 cm) long. Align rods, pinch them together at center. Press rods onto center of spider's flat side, for legs. Arrange legs as desired; smooth seams with toothpick. Insert screw eye into belly. Prop spider body on aluminum foil; bake with other shapes.

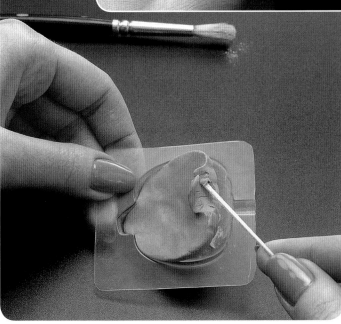

8 Load small amount of baby powder on artist's brush; dust candy mold. Estimate amount of clay needed to fill candy mold about half full; roll ball. Press ball into general shape; push into mold. Insert toothpick carefully along edge; gently pry clay from mold.

(Continued)

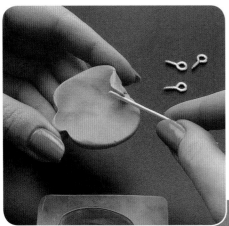

9 Smooth nicked areas, using toothpick; draw with toothpick tip to accentuate details, if desired. Gently insert screw eye at top of shape. Place shapes on baking sheet; bake, following manufacturer's directions.

10 Roll clay flat on clean Formica surface. Cut designs, using cookie cutters or knife. Add surface details, using toothpick. Gently poke hole at least ⅛" (3 mm) from top of design. Place shapes on baking sheet; drape over aluminum foil props, if desired. Bake, following manufacturer's directions.

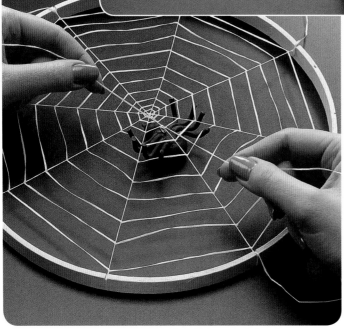

11 Accent baked shapes with paint, if desired. Knot strands of floss to screw eyes and holes in shapes. Attach spider to web. Hang other shapes from web, trimming floss to various lengths. Tie four hanger tails to small plastic ring for hanging.

Shape Variations

Blend two colors of clay well to achieve new colors or partially blend colors to get marblized surface variations.

Make glow-in-the-dark forms that float mysteriously overhead when the lights go out. Use Fimo Nite-Glo clay. Or highlight areas of colorful shapes with glow-in-the-dark paint.

Tie wired felt shapes (page 216) to web with invisible thread.

Tie small purchased ornaments to web.

SCARECROW WALL HANGING

Handsome Mr. Scarecrow has banned all crows from the pumpkin patch in this three-dimensional wall hanging. Some embellishments are included as you piece him together; others, added just before hanging him on a branch, provide lots of ways to make this banner uniquely your own.

The banner is a collection of easily pieced blocks; large background rectangles make it quick to assemble. Fabric scraps are suitable for the entire scarecrow and the pumpkins. Use ¼" (6 mm) seam allowances throughout, stitching at 12 to 15 stitches per inch (2.5 cm).

You Will Need

- ¼ yd. (0.25 m) fabric, for background
- ⅛ yd. (0.15 m) each of five fabrics, or assorted scraps, for scarecrow face, clothing, and pumpkins
- ¼ yd. (0.25 m) fabric, for border
- raffia
- jute twine
- ⅝ yd. (0.6 m) fusible batting
- ⅝ yd. (0.6 m) fabric, for backing
- embroidery floss as desired
- permanent markers, optional
- decorative buttons
- fusible web, ⅜" (1 cm) wide
- wood fence; assorted wood shapes, optional
- tea bag and assorted paints, optional
- glue gun and glue sticks, optional
- branch, about 30" (76 cm) long

How to Make a Scarecrow Wall Hanging

1 Press two pants rectangles in half, wrong sides together, to measure 1⅞" × 4½" (4.7 × 11.5 cm). Pin to right side of large rectangle A; place folds near center and align raw edges at top and sides. Place third pants rectangle, right side down, over legs. Stitch across top, securing both legs; turn third pants rectangle up.

Cutting Directions

From the background fabric, cut fourteen 1" (2.5 cm) squares; cut two pieces, using the template (page 238). Cut five small rectangles; two 1¼" × 2½" (3.2 × 6.5 cm), one 2½" × 1½" (6.5 × 3.8 cm), one 2½" × 2" (6.5 × 5 cm), and one 1" × 3½" (2.5 × 9 cm). Cut three large rectangles; cut A 4" × 5" (10 × 12.5 cm), cut B 7" × 11½" (18 × 29.3 cm), cut C 6½" × 14½" (16.3 × 36.8 cm). Cut two strips; one 16½" × 2" (41.8 × 5 cm) and one 16½" × 3" (41.8 × 7.5 cm).

Cut two 3¾" × 4½" (9.5 × 11.5 cm) and one 4" × 2½" (10 × 6.5 cm) rectangles from the pants fabric.

Cut one 4" (10 cm) square and one 9" × 3½" (23 × 9 cm) rectangle from the shirt fabric.

Cut one 2½" (6.5 cm) square from the head fabric.

From the hat fabric, cut one 4" × 2" (10 × 5 cm) rectangle; cut one piece, using the hat template (page 238).

From the pumpkin fabric, cut one 2½" (6.5 cm) square and two rectangles; one 2½" × 3½" (6.5 × 9 cm) and one 2½" × 2" (6.5 × 5 cm). Also cut six 3" (7.5 cm) squares and two 3" × 3¾" (7.5 × 9.5 cm) rectangles for padded pumpkins.

Cut seven strips; two 3½" × 18½" (9 × 47.3 cm), two 3½" × 22½" (9 × 57.2 cm) and three 3" × 20" (7.5 × 51 cm) from border fabric.

(Continued)

2 Pin 1" (2.5 cm) background squares to bottom corners of head square, right sides together. Stitch diagonally across small squares, corner to corner. Trim seam allowances to ¼" (6 mm); press to make square. Stitch matching background rectangle to each side of head, right sides together; press seam allowances toward background.

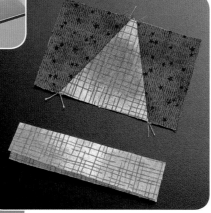

3 Stitch background sections to hat triangle, right sides together, to form 2½" × 4" (6.5 × 10 cm) block; press. Press hat rectangle in half lengthwise, wrong sides together, for brim.

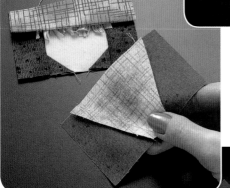

4 Cut raffia pieces about 1" (2.5 cm) long; arrange across top of head. Place brim and then lower edge of raffia, right sides down and raw edges even with top and sides of head block; pin. Stitch; turn hat up.

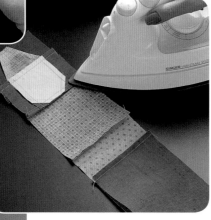

5 Stitch shirt square to top of pants. Stitch head block to shirt top. Press scarecrow block; press seam allowances away from head and legs.

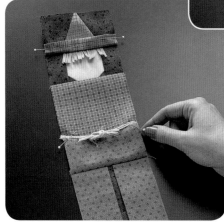

6 Turn brim up about ½" (1.3 cm); pin at sides of block. Knot pieces of twine for belt; pin at waist sides.

7 Pin 1" (2.5 cm) background squares to each corner of three small pumpkin pieces. Stitch; trim and press as in step 2, opposite.

8 Assemble the pumpkin block, using three pumpkin squares and three small background pieces, following diagram on page 238; stitch horizontal seams first, then vertical seams.

9 Stitch large rectangle B to upper edge of pumpkin block, right sides together; press. Stitch block to left side of scarecrow block. Stitch large rectangle C to right side of scarecrow block; catch ends of belt and hat brim in seams.

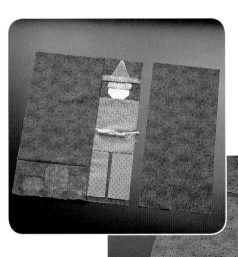

10 Pin a few short raffia pieces to hat top. Stitch background strips to top and bottom of pieced unit, catching raffia in top seam. Press entire block; press last seams toward pieced unit.

(Continued)

11 Fold sleeve in half lengthwise; press. Press raw edges under ¼" (6 mm). Place second fold over head block and shirt seam, centering sleeve on body; sleeve will cover face. Pin; stitch on foldline. Press sleeve down.

12 Stitch short border strips to sides of pieced unit; press seam allowances toward borders. Stitch long border strips to top and bottom of unit; press. Bordered unit should measure 22½" × 24½" (57.2 × 62.3 cr

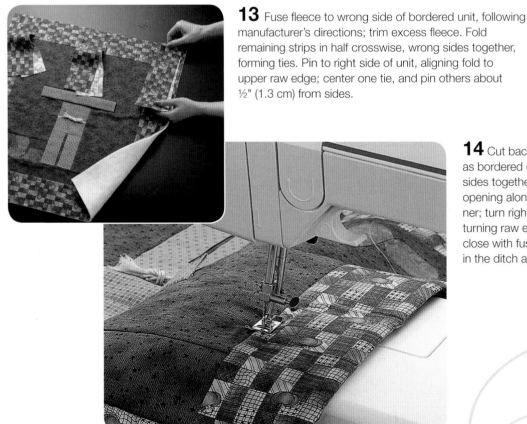

13 Fuse fleece to wrong side of bordered unit, following manufacturer's directions; trim excess fleece. Fold remaining strips in half crosswise, wrong sides together, forming ties. Pin to right side of unit, aligning fold to upper raw edge; center one tie, and pin others about ½" (1.3 cm) from sides.

14 Cut backing fabric to same size as bordered unit. Stitch to unit, right sides together, leaving 6" (15 cm) opening along lower edge. Trim corner; turn right side out. Press lightly, turning raw edges in at opening; close with fusible web strip. Stitch in the ditch around border.

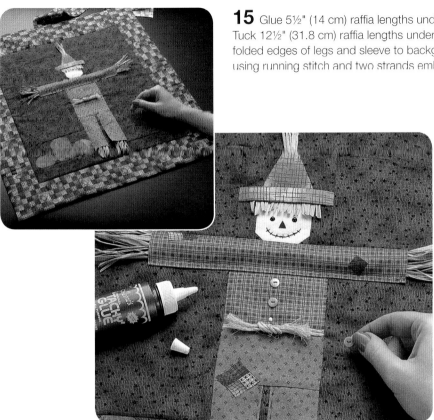

15 Glue 5½" (14 cm) raffia lengths under pants legs. Tuck 12½" (31.8 cm) raffia lengths under sleeve. Secure folded edges of legs and sleeve to background, using running stitch and two strands embroidery floss.

16 Embellish scarecrow as desired. Draw or embroider face. Fuse small patches to clothing. Add buttons for clothing details.

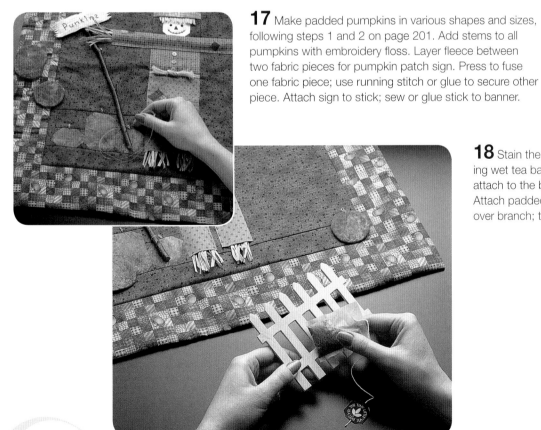

17 Make padded pumpkins in various shapes and sizes, following steps 1 and 2 on page 201. Add stems to all pumpkins with embroidery floss. Layer fleece between two fabric pieces for pumpkin patch sign. Press to fuse one fabric piece; use running stitch or glue to secure other piece. Attach sign to stick; sew or glue stick to banner.

18 Stain the wooden shapes, using wet tea bag, or paint as desired; attach to the banner as desired. Attach padded pumpkins. Knot ties over branch; trim excess length.

PICTURE FRAMES

Display photos of your favorite Halloween ghouls and guys in wooden picture frames you make yourself. Design any shape, allowing adequate space beyond the opening for a backing board or use the patterns on pages 231 and 232. Stand frames with a level bottom edge on a table. Plan symmetrical designs for hanging frames on a wall, or adjust the placement of the hanger to allow the frame to hang straight. Cut openings to fit standard 5" × 7" (12.5 × 18 cm) or 4" × 6" (10 × 15 cm) photos. Paint, stain, stencil, and embellish the frames in a variety of ways. Use Paper Etch for a wood-burned effect, or glue wood cutouts, buttons, or polymer clay shapes to the frame surface.

How to Make a Picture Frame

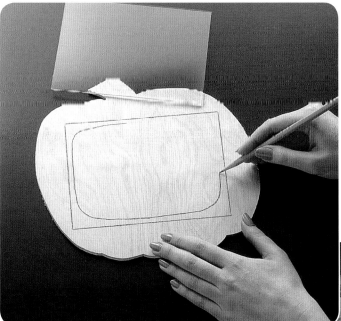

1 Trace desired outline on board; cut out shape, using jigsaw or coping saw. Center glass on back of board, near lower edge and parallel to sides; trace outer edge. Mark cutting line for opening at least ¼" (6 mm) inside traced line, shaping as desired.

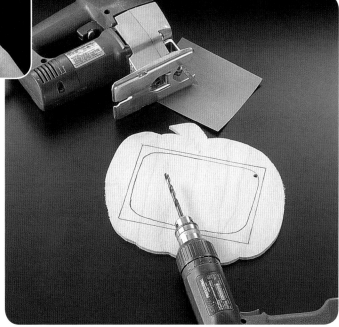

2 Drill hole for inserting saw blade just inside marked line; more than one hole may be necessary. Cut away opening, using jigsaw. Sand opening and outer edges, using 220-grit sandpaper.

(Continued)

You Will Need

- finish-grade ¼" (6 mm) plywood or poplar board
- glass, 5" × 7" (12.5 × 18 cm)
- drill and ¼" drill bit
- coping saw or jigsaw
- hardboard, ⅛" (3 mm) thick
- 220-grit sandpaper
- wood glue
- craft sticks, for spacers
- drive-in picture hanger, for hanging frame
- easel, 5" × 7" (12.5 × 18 cm) for standing frame
- materials for finishing and decorative frames, such as acrylic paints, water-based wood stain, Paper Etch, aerosol acrylic sealer, wood cutouts, polymer clay shapes, or Halloween buttons
- hot glue gun and glue sticks, optional

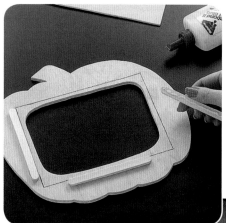

3 Cut backing from hardboard, allowing ½" (1.3 cm) on three sides to extend beyond glass; trim corners, if necessary. Glue two craft sticks together for each spacer; cut to desired length. Secure spacers to frame back just beyond bottom and side glass lines, using wood glue.

4 Secure backing over spacers, using wood glue; align sides and lower edge of backing to outer edges of spacers. Weight with books until dry.

5 Glue easel to back of standing frame, with lower edge of easel near lower edge of frame. Trim easel, if necessary. Or install picture hanger at top center of backing for symmetrical hanging frame; install a hanger at each upper corner for asymmetrical frames. Paint or decorate frame as desired.

Tips for Decorating Frames

Paint frame, using craft acrylic paints; seal with aerosol acrylic sealer, if desired. Attach wooden cutouts, Halloween charms, or buttons, using hot glue. Snip off button shank, using wire cutter. Make polymer clay shapes (pages 169–170). Sand back flat, if necessary. Adhere to surface of frame, using hot glue gun.

Draw design features, using Paper Etch; follow the manufacturer's directions. Stain frame, using light-colored water-based wood stain. Finish with aerosol acrylic sealer.

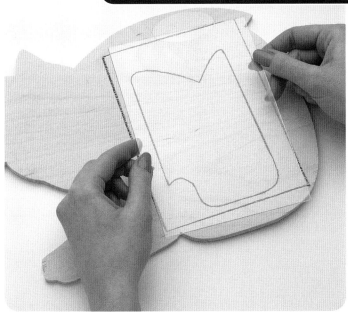

Shape photo opening as part of design, if desired. Or cut two small openings.

HAUNTED BIRDHOUSES

Watch for friendly spirits to move into this once lovely old mansion. Simply transform a birdhouse and set it on a small hill with a rickety picket fence; the spirits will beckon you from behind shuttered windows and welcome you at the door.

Choose from many birdhouse styles available at craft stores for just the mansion you want. A tall, slim house resembles a stately mansion; one with slanted sides appears empty and tumbledown. Select from special shapes like a barn or log cabin, or look for interesting details like tiered roofs and multiple openings.

Use a crackle medium to imitate old, weathered paint, and age the mansion with a light rubbing of dark stain. Draw unique features, such as mullions and faces on the windows, or add slats and knobs to the shutters, using fine tip brushes or opaque markers. Hang shutters at odd angles and stretch purchased cobwebs between jutting details, if desired.

Create three-dimensional inhabitants for the house, following the directions for wired felt place cards (page 216). Purchase precut wood shapes or dollhouse miniatures to decorate the sides of the house.

Consider various ways to decorate the mansion's hillside landscape. Build a tumbledown fence, add barren trees and tombstones, and scatter small leaves, if desired.

You Will Need

- craft birdhouse
- drill; ½" (1.3 cm) drill bit
- ½" (1.3 cm) dowel
- wood glue
- acrylic paints, artist's brushes
- crackle medium
- dark stain; rag; rubber gloves, optional
- balsa wood, ¹⁄₁₆" and ⅛" (1.5 and 3 mm) thick
- straightedge, mat knife, cutting surface
- 1 yd. (0.95 m) acetate lining fabric, black
- embellishments as desired; hot glue gun

How to Make a Haunted Birdhouse

1 Drill hole through birdhouse roof at desired chimney location, using ½" drill bit; drill hole at slight angle if tumbledown chimney is desired. Cut 2" (5 cm) dowel length. Apply glue to inner rim of hole; secure dowel in place. Allow glue to dry.

2 Paint birdhouse with base colors as desired. Apply second coat, allow to dry. Apply even, light coat of crackle medium; allow to set, following manufacturer's directions.

3 Apply single coat of contrasting paint; paint will crackle soon after it is applied. Allow to dry. Rub stain lightly over entire house, using cloth; apply stain more heavily to some areas to show extra wear.

(Continued)

4 Cut windows in desired shapes and sized from ¹⁄₁₆"
(1.5 mm) balsa wood. Cut shutters from ⅛" (3 mm)
balsa wood. Paint and stain as desired; allow to dry.
Attach windows and shutters, using hot glue. Allow to
hang at odd angles, if desired.

5 Decorate the front entry as desired;
position a wired felt shape (page 216)
in entry hole. Suspend another wired felt
shape over house, wrapping wire around
chimney or eave. Add other embellishments
as desired.

6 Form hill, using box and aluminum foil; tape crumpled
foil near edges, and slope to table surface. Cover hill
with fleece or batting.

7 Wet black fabric; twist and roll
into ball. Allow to dry. Unroll fabric,
and drape over hill; tuck raw edges
under. Place house on hill. Make
picket fence as shown opposite;
position fence around house.

8 Embellish hill as desired. Purchase trees or make trees
from twigs. Cut small headstones from balsa wood; spray
with fleckstone paint, if desired, and secure to front of
small rocks, using hot glue. Attach cobwebs, if desired.

How to Make a Picket Fence

1 Use scissors to cut near center of craft stick tip. Break stick in half lengthwise; allow break to follow wood grain for irregular shapes. Use warped and knotted sticks for added interest. Full lengths will be used for horizontal rails; broken sticks for vertical stiles

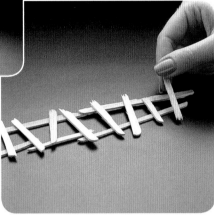

2 Position two uneven rows of rails on surface, about 1" (2.5 cm) apart, so total length is 3" to 4" (7.5 to 10 cm) longer than house side. Repeat for each fence section and gate. Arrange stiles on rails at various angles. Use short stiles for broken sections; avoid placing stiles at end of rails.

3 Glue stiles to rails, one at a time, using hot glue.

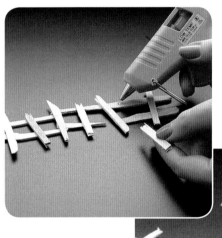

You Will Need

- craft sticks, scissors
- hot glue gun
- mat knife, optional
- ⁵⁄₁₆" (7.5 mm) dowel, one ³⁄₈" (1 cm) button plug for each fence post
- paint, stain, applicators

4 Cut 2¼" (6 cm) dowel length for each post; glue button plug to top of each post. Glue posts to rails at corners and ends. Trim excess glue from fence, if necessary, using mat knife. Paint or stain as desired.

WOODEN SHELF SITTERS

This collection of shelf sitters will happily watch over your holiday observations. Create your favorite characters and scatter them throughout the house or gather them together to impart their own special magic.

Purchase inexpensive 2 × 2 nominal lumber, which actually measures 1¾" × 1¾" (4.5 × 4.5 cm), for their bodies. Use various precut wood shapes, such as square blocks, round balls, and inverted pears for their heads. Join shelf sitter parts after drilling holes in adjacent pieces; clamp small pieces to a work surface to ensure centered and parallel holes, and for safety.

Consider a character's special traits before embellishing. Purchase small precut wood shapes for unique details. "Dress" shelf sitters in appropriate colors and give them cheerful faces, using acrylic paints. Use simple modeling techniques or purchase molds to form clay hands, boots, or special details. Suspend hands and foot inside sleeves and pants that require only a few seams.

You Will Need

- 2 × 2 nominal pine
- 1¼" (3.2 cm) square wood block, for head
- ⅝" × ¾" (1.5 × 2 cm) spool, for neck
- ³⁄₁₆" (4.5 mm) dowel
- saw, clamp
- drill; ⁵⁄₁₆", ³⁄₁₆" drill bits; masking tape
- acrylic paints, colors as desired
- two ¼" (6 mm) wood blocks, for neck nodes
- wood glue
- fake fur scrap, for hair, optional
- polymer clay, craft mold for 1½" (3.8 cm) hands, baby powder, artist's knife, tooth-pick, small screw eyes, baking sheet
- ⅛ yd. (0.15 m) fabric, safety pin
- ¾ yd. (0.7 m) cording

Cutting Directions

Cut one 4" (10 cm) piece of 2 × 2 pine board, for the body.

Cut one 1½" (3.8 cm) piece of dowel, for the neck.

Cut one 5" × 15" (12.5 × 38 cm) fabric strip, for the legs. Cut one 5" × 9" (12.5 × 23 cm) fabric strip, for the arms. Cut cording in two lengths of 11" and 16" (28 and 40.5 cm).

How to Make a Frankenstein Shelf Sitter

1 Mark center of one end on body and head. Drill holes to ⅜" (1 cm) depth, using ³⁄₁₆" drill bit; wrap masking tape around drill bit as guide for depth. Mark two points on body front, ⅜" (1 cm) up from bottom and in from side. Mark point on body side, ¾" (2 cm) down from top and in from back. Drill holes through body at marks, using ⁵⁄₁₆" drill bit.

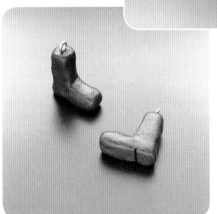

2 Paint body, head, neck, and two neck nodes. Allow to dry; paint facial features. Paint hair, or glue fake fur scrap on head. Glue neck nodes to each side of neck. Glue dowel in each end hole. Allow to dry.

3 Soften clay for boot. Roll clay ball into fat 2" (5 cm)-long cylinder. Fold one-third of cylinder under, forming boot front. Shape boot as desired; mark heel with knife. Insert screw eye into top as shown. Repeat for second boot.

(Continued)

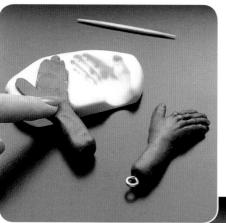

4 Soften clay for hands. Press clay ball into approximate mold shape; place in lightly dusted mold. Push clay into fingertips; push clay beyond mold edges, and extend arm about 1" (2.5 cm) beyond wrist. Gently lift hand from mold; remove excess clay, using knife tip. Roll toothpick along edges to smooth; use tip to add or accentuate details. Gently cup palm. Insert screw eyes into arm ends. Bake boots and hands, following manufacturer's directions.

5 Turn under ¼" (6 mm) on each short end of fabric strip; edgestitch. Fold strip in half lengthwise, right sides together; stitch ¼" (6 mm) seam. Turn tube right side out, using safety pin. Repeat with other strip. Gather ends slightly, using hand stitches.

6 Thread short cord through short tube, using safety pin. Insert tube through side hole, for sleeves. Tie cord ends to hands, adjusting position of hand in the sleeve as desired; trim the cord. Thread long cord through long tube for pants; insert legs through holes from back. Secure boots.

Variations for Shelf Sitters

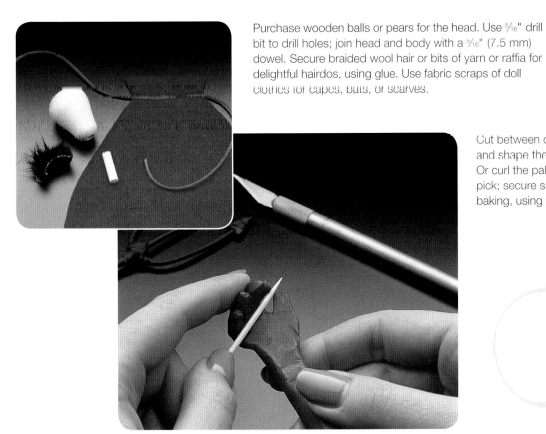

Purchase wooden balls or pears for the head. Use ⁵⁄₁₆" drill bit to drill holes; join head and body with a ⁵⁄₁₆" (7.5 mm) dowel. Secure braided wool hair or bits of yarn or raffia for delightful hairdos, using glue. Use fabric scraps of doll clothes for capes, hats, or scarves.

Cut between clay fingers; separate and shape them slightly as desired. Or curl the palm gently around toothpick; secure small item in hand after baking, using all-purpose adhesive.

Sew a third fabric tube for a tail; knot end around leg fabric at back. To pose a character's arms, legs, or tail, substitute chenille stems for the cording.

Apply transparent stain, instead of paint, to allow the wood grain to show on natural characters, such as scarecrows and pumpkins.

Throw a Party

Worms
and
Beetles

Eye of
Newt

Dragon's Br
Stew

Fill cauldron ha
full with Beetle
Add two handful
of white worms. Sti

HARLEQUIN TABLE RUNNER

This easy-to-sew pointed harlequin table runner makes a beautiful backdrop for Halloween appliqué motifs. The finished size is about 51" × 18½" (129.5 × 47.3 cm). Lengthen the runner, if desired, by adding diagonal rows of blocks.

This runner uses the easiest of sewing methods. Cut fabric squares and strips with a rotary cutter and mat, for greatest efficiency. A 6" (15 cm)-wide transparent straightedge makes it easy to cut accurately. Stitch ¼" (6 mm) seams, using a short stitch length.

Simple Halloween appliqués are fused to the runner. You may prefer to substitute pumpkins, flying witches, ghosts, or ravens for the black cat. Edgestitch around the appliqués to give them interesting dimension.

How to Make a Harlequin Table Runner

1 Stitch six A squares to six B squares, right sides together, stitching along one side. Stitch four remaining A squares to opposite sides of the same B squares, right sides together. You will have two A–B rows and four A–B–A rows.

2 Arrange rows diagonally. Place triangles at ends of rows as shown. Stitch triangles to ends of rows. Press all seam allowances toward A squares.

3 Stitch the rows together; seam allowances alternate in opposite directions at intersecting seams. Press; avoid stretching bias edges of triangles. Measure sides; cut two border strips equal to shorter measurement plus ½" (1.3 cm).

You Will Need

- ⅜ yd. (0.35 m) fabric A, for outer rows of squares
- ¼ yd. (0.25 m) fabric B, for center squares
- ¼ yd. (0.25 m) fabric C, for outer triangles
- ¾ yd. (0.7 m) fabric, for backing
- ¼ yd. (0.25 m) fabric, for border
- batting, about 20" × 54" (51 × 137 cm)
- ¼ yd. (0.25 m) black fabric, for cats, or suitable fabric scraps, for appliqués
- paper-backed fusible web
- straightedge

Cutting Directions

Cut ten 6" (15 cm) squares from fabric A, six 6" (15 cm) squares from fabric B, and four 6⅜" (16 cm) squares from fabric C. Cut fabric C squares diagonally to make eight triangles

Cut four 2" (5 cm) strips across the width of the border fabric.

(Continued)

4 Pin border strips to sides. Stitch, easing as necessary; press seams toward border. Lay straight edge along diagonal end of runner; trim border strip end. Repeat on remaining ends of border strips.

5 Cut border strip equal to length of one diagonal edge plus ½" (1.3 cm). Pin strip to runner, aligning one end to runner point; strip extends past side strip. Stitch; press. Repeat for adjoining diagonal edge. Repeat for opposite end. Trim the end strips even with side strips.

6 Trace Halloween motifs (page 235) on paper side of fusible web; fuse to motif fabric, following manufacturer's directions. Cut out motifs; remove paper, and fuse to runner.

7 Seam backing fabric as necessary to measure about 20" × 54" (51 × 137 cm). Cut fabric the shape of the runner, using pieced top as pattern. Layer pieced top and backing, right sides together and all edges aligned, over batting; pin all around.

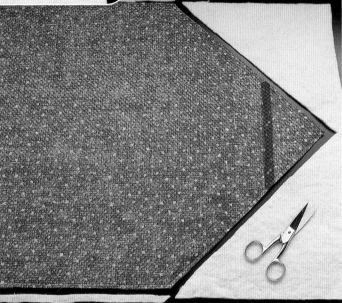

8 Stitch around outer edge, pivoting at corners; leave 6" (15 cm) opening on one side. Trim batting close to stitching; trim even with fabric at opening. Turn. Press lightly, tucking seam allowances in; pin opening closed.

9 Edgestitch around border. Stitch in the ditch between rows of blocks and around border. Edgestitch around appliqué motifs.

PUMPKIN TABLE LINENS

This easy-to-sew set of table linens clearly emphasizes the traditional Halloween pumpkin, and it is just as appropriate for the whole harvest season. Create the entire set or select your favorite parts to delight your dinner guests.

Padded placemats are embellished with a stem and leaves. Top-stitched pumpkin ribs and leaf veins add interesting dimension. An optional paper twist tendril is removed for laundering.

For simplicity and minimal expense, the table runner is made from the full width of fabric. The runner and napkins feature fused appliqués. They may be embellished with hand sewing or fabric paint. Allow paints to dry 24 hours before use and 72 hours before laundering. Any raffia bows or tassels at the points of the table runner should be removed before laundering.

Placemats, table runner, and napkins (opposite) set a cozy country table for daily family meals. Or bring them out for special autumn occasions. Surprise your guests with spiderweb coasters.

You Will Need

For One Table Runner, Four Placemats, Four Napkins, and Four Coasters:

- ½ yd. (0.5 m) fabric, for table runner
- 1⅝ yd. (1.5 m) fabric, for pumpkin shell
- ⅜ yd. (0.35 m) fabric, for leaves and stems
- polyester or cotton batting; 28" × 38" (71 × 96.5 cm) for placemats and 5" (12.5 cm) square scraps for coasters
- tracing paper, 14" × 19" (35.5 × 48.5 cm)
- erasable marking pen or pencil
- paper-backed fusible web
- fusible web, ⅜" (1 cm) wide
- green paper twist with wire core, optional
- 1 yd. (0.95 m) fabric, for napkins
- embroidery floss, orange, green, black, optional
- dimensional fabric paints, optional
- ¼ yd. (0.25 m) fabric or 5" (12.5 cm) square scraps, for coasters
- raffia, plastic spiders, optional

Cutting Decorations

For the table runner, fold the fabric crosswise, aligning the selvages. Trim both edges as necessary so they are at right angles to the selvages. Cut away the selvages.

For the placemats, fold tracing paper into fourths; unfold. Trace the pattern (page 230) in one quadrant. Refold the paper; cut on the marked line through all layers to make a full pattern.

Cut the pumpkin shells; eight from fabric, four from batting.

Cut 3½" × 5" (9 × 12.5 cm) rectangles for the stems; eight from fabric, four from batting.

Cut 5" (12.5 cm) squares for leaves; sixteen from fabric, eight from batting.

For the napkins, cut four 18" (46 cm) squares.

For the coasters, cut eight 5" (12.5 cm) fabric squares and four 5" (12.5 cm) batting squares.

How to Make a Pumpkin Placemat

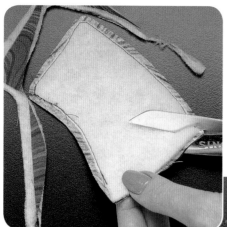

1 Trace and cut out stem pattern (page 230). Transfer pattern outline to wrong side of one fabric rectangle. Layer two rectangles, right sides together, over batting rectangle, with pattern outline on top. Stitch on marked line, leaving bottom open. Trim batting close to stitching; trim fabric to scant ¼" (6 mm) from stitching and on bottom line. Clip curves. Turn right side out; press lightly. Edgestitch seamlines.

2 Trace, cut, and transfer leaf pattern, as in step 1; cut 2" (5 cm) slit at center of one shape. Layer fabric squares and batting, as in step 1. Stitch along entire line. Trim batting and fabric, as in step 1; slip at pivot points and along curves. Turn leaf right side out through slit; press lightly. Slip 2¼" (6 cm) fusible web strip inside slit; fuse closed. Stitch leaf veins. Edgestitch, stretching edge slightly to curve. Repeat for second leaf.

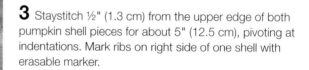

3 Staystitch ½" (1.3 cm) from the upper edge of both pumpkin shell pieces for about 5" (12.5 cm), pivoting at indentations. Mark ribs on right side of one shell with erasable marker.

4 Layer pumpkin shells, right sides together, over batting; pin. Stitch ½" (1.3 cm) seam allowance; backstitch at each end of staystitching, leaving 5" (12.5 cm) opening.

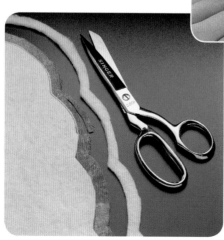

5 Trim batting close to stitching and even with staystitching along opening. Trim fabric seam allowance to scant ¼" (6 mm); leave opening untrimmed. Clip to stitching at each pivot point; clip all around shell at ½" (1.3 cm) intervals. Turn; press lightly, turning under seam allowances of opening.

6 Insert stem ¾" (2 cm) into opening; pin. Edgestitch placemat, catching stem and closing opening. Stitch on marked rib lines. Tack leaves loosely to top of pumpkin. Wrap paper twist around pencil to create tendril, if desired. Slip tendril under leaf, between tacking.

How to Make a Table Runner

1 Press under ¼" (6 mm) twice on long sides; stitch to make double-fold hems.

2 Fold runner in half lengthwise, right sides together; pin ends. Stitch ¼" (6 mm) seams at both ends. Press seams open. Turn right side out, and position seam at center of runner; press diagonal folds.

3 Trace medium pumpkin and stem twice on paper side of paper-backed fusible web. Fuse to fabrics, following manufacturer's directions. Cut out pumpkins and stems; fuse near table runner ends.

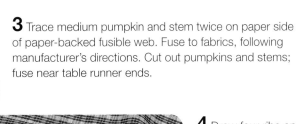

4 Draw four ribs on pumpkins with erasable marker. Hand-stitch running stitches along ribs, using one strand of embroidery floss. Backstitch tendrils, using three strands of floss. Or outline pumpkins, ribs, and stems with fabric paint. Pin raffia bow or tassels at points, if desired.

How to Make a Halloween Napkin

1 Press under ½" (1.3 cm) on each side of the fabric square. Unfold corner; fold diagonally so pressed folds are aligned. Press diagonal fold; trim corner.

2 Fold raw edges under ¼" (6 mm). Press double-fold hem in place. Stitch close to inner fold, pivoting at mitered corners.

3 Fuse and embellish small pumpkin and stem near napkin corner, as for table runner, steps 3 and 4.

How to Make a Coaster

1 Draw 4½" (11.5 cm) circle on wrong side of one fabric square. Slit fabric for about 1½" (3.8 cm) at circle center. Layer fabrics, right sides together, on batting. Stitch on line.

2 Trim batting close to stitching. Trim fabric to scant ¼" (6 mm); clip seam allowances at ½" (1.3 cm) intervals. Turn, press, and fuse slit closed as for pumpkin leaf (page 198).

3 Stitch web spokes from edge to edge, using contrasting thread; backstitch at edge. Stitch three circles of connecting web lines as shown. Tack plastic spider to coaster side, if desired.

PAINTED GLASS SERVERS

Serve Halloween treats on a variety of hand-painted glass dishes. Use basic techniques and special acrylic paints developed for use on glass or tile, or mix a glass medium into acrylic craft paints.

Select heat-set glass and tile paints to decorate tempered glass dishes. Select air-dry enamels or modify craft paints when it is not possible to determine if the glass is tempered; air-dry ten days before use.

Painting Tips

Avoid painting surfaces that will come in contact with food or be put in mouths, even if the paints are non-toxic. Experiment with paints to determine their translucency; modified craft paints and some glass paint brands are more opaque.

Plan a design on a paper pattern, if desired. Consider how the dish will be viewed; paint mirror images on the underside of plates and trays or when letters and designs will be viewed from inside containers like bowls and stemware.

Create a stencil for very clean edges; limit stencil designs to a single color, as stencil adhesives may lift the paints. Or paint designs freehand. Apply paint using artist's brushes and household items to achieve a carefree look. Apply paint using sponges for a dappled effect. Allow paint to dry thoroughly between coats.

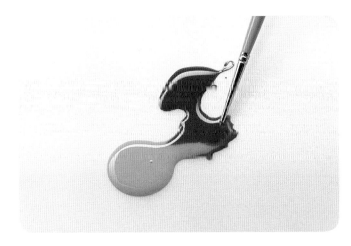

Create unique colors by blending colors of any one manufacturer; avoid blending colors from different manufacturers.

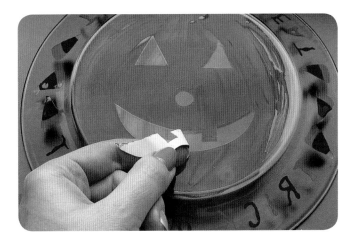

Mask design areas, using self-adhesive vinyl. Remove vinyl immediately after painting.

Apply thin lines of paint using accent liner, or fill craft bottle with paint and use small-tip cap.

You Will Need

- glass serving dishes
- paper; tape
- isopropyl alcohol, lint-free cloth
- air-dry or heat-set glass and tile paints, or acrylic paints and glass medium; brushes
- newspaper, wood blocks
- small dowels; craft bottles with tip set, optional
- removable tape, self-adhesive vinyl, mat knife, and cutting surface, for stencil painting
- cellulose or sea sponges, for sponge painting

How to Paint a Design

1 Mark general shape of glass item on paper; trace outer edges of nearly flat items, or draw rectangle with dimensions equal to height and circumference of curved items. Draw design within shape. Wash glass well in hot, soapy water; dry. Wipe glass with isopropyl alcohol, using lint-free cloth. Place pattern facedown on right side of item, positioning as desired. Cut the pattern as necessary, lapping paper to fit item without distorting design details; tape.

2 Turn item over, or rest it on its side; place on newspaper. Apply as many foreground colors as possible; apply second coat, if necessary. Allow paint to dry thoroughly.

3 Paint adjacent colors, lapping first colors slightly; apply second coats, if necessary. Dry thoroughly. Continue until entire pattern is painted.

4 Dip brush handle tip into paint to apply small, slightly irregular dots of color. Use dowel ends of various sizes for larger, more perfect paint circles. Cut motifs from cellulose sponges. Dip sponge into paint puddle; blot on newspaper to remove excess paint. Press sponge evenly on flat surfaces, or roll sponge across curved surfaces.

5 Dip sea sponge into paint; blot on newspaper. Dab paint on glass, turning and rotating sponge to avoid repetition of sponge pattern.

6 Prop glass on wood blocks and paint entire bottom or outside of dish, if desired. Cure, following manufacturer's directions. Apply two coats of clear gloss or satin glaze to improve durability of painted designs; allow one hour between coats. Cure well before washing.

How to Make and Use a Stencil

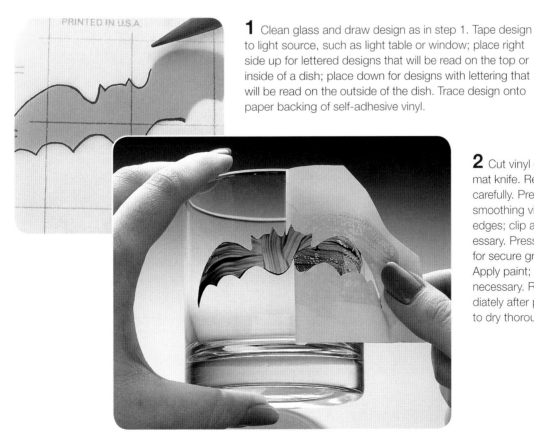

1 Clean glass and draw design as in step 1. Tape design to light source, such as light table or window; place right side up for lettered designs that will be read on the top or inside of a dish; place down for designs with lettering that will be read on the outside of the dish. Trace design onto paper backing of self-adhesive vinyl.

2 Cut vinyl on design lines, using mat knife. Remove paper backing carefully. Press vinyl to the glass, smoothing vinyl from center to outer edges; clip and lap vinyl where necessary. Press all vinyl edges firmly for secure grip; avoid touching glass. Apply paint; apply second coat, if necessary. Remove stencil immediately after painting. Allow paint to dry thoroughly.

TREAT BAG INVITATIONS

Deliver these invitations to your guests in person, or if they're away, leave a bag on a doorknob to brighten their return. Advise them to bring the invitation to the party and they'll go home with a bag full of treats!

Select small gift or craft bags that have handles, or cut handles in ordinary lunch bags. This is a fun project for children of all ages; just gather the materials and each invitation will be unique.

Write party details on the back of the bag or on heavy paper trimmed to fit inside.

Cutting Ways to Decorate an Invitation

Mark bag for handle 1" (2.5 cm) down from top center; mark 2½" (6.5 cm) from top and 1" (2.5 cm) in from each side; draw half circle to connect marks. Place bag over heavy cardboard; cut through both layers, using mat knife. Or cut handle, using scissors. Trace handle of first bag on remaining bags, if desired.

Mark silhouette shape on bag front. Insert firm cardboard into bag to prevent cutting bag back. Cut out shape, using mat knife. Insert construction paper backing, trimmed slightly smaller than bag; secure with glue.

You Will Need

For Cutting and Stamping:
- mat knife, scissors, cardboard
- construction paper, markers
- artist's eraser or printing block, tracing paper, transfer paper, for making a stamp
- purchased rubber stamps, optional
- stamp pads

For Fabric Collage:
- prequilted fabric; or fabric, batting, and muslin
- sewing machine, or hand needle and thread
- shears, regular or pinking
- fabric scraps, fabric paints, and embellishments as desired

Purchase Halloween stickers for quick-and-easy treat bag invitations.

How to Create a Fabric Collage

1 Measure bag front; subtract ¾" (2 cm) from each dimension to determine fabric rectangle size. Mark rectangle on fabric, using pencil lightly. Repeat for each invitation, drawing rectangles about ½" (1.3 cm) apart. To make your own quilted fabric, sandwich batting between marked fabric and muslin; pin layers together.

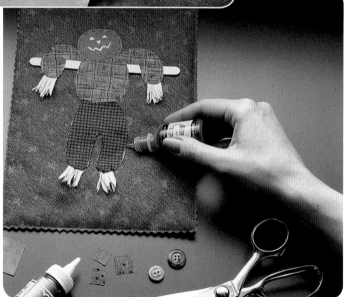

2 Stitch fabric layers together along rectangle lines. Cut rectangles just outside stitching; use pinking shears, if desired. Layer a collage of fabric shapes on rectangle to make a Halloween picture. Secure shapes with craft glue or hand stitches; cover raw edges or add details, using fabric paints, if desired. Embellish with fabric trims, buttons, and hand stitches as desired. Attach collage to bag, using glue.

How to Cut and Use Stamps

1 Trace design onto paper. Transfer to smooth side of artist's eraser or printing block, using transfer paper. Cut ⅛" (3 mm) deep along design lines, using mat knife.

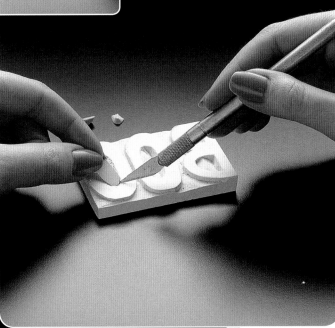

2 Remove large background area by cutting horizontally through eraser edge and up to design cuts. Cut and remove narrow spaces within design by cutting down at an angle along lines.

3 Insert the cardboard into bag between top layer and bottom folds and seams. Press stamp firmly onto stamp pad; lift and repeat until design is evenly coated. Press straight down onto the bag, using even pressure. Color the design, using markers, if desired.

FOAM TREAT CUPS

Let party guests create personal dinner companions when they make these easy and inexpensive foam treat cups.

Recycle assorted food cans for the cup. Consider shallow tuna cans for seated figures holding small candies. Use mandarin orange cans for short bodies or heads holding individually wrapped pieces, or use soup cans for standing figures holding stick candy and small bags.

How to Make a Foam Treat Cup

Purchase thin sheets of colored foam to cover the cans. Cut various shapes for the bottom and back pieces; use decorative-edge scissors to cut creative details, such as lace edging on a witch's petticoat or spikes on a dragon's tail, if desired. Secure the main pieces before the party starts if the guests are young or if there are lots of other things to do.

Provide additional foam pieces and colored markers so party guests may decorate the silhouettes as they like. Layer colors by cutting desired shapes first, or trim a larger piece after it is glued to the basic shape, using the basic shape as a pattern. Use a paper punch to cut perfect holes for a ghost's eyes or to add spots to a monster. Insert small pieces into pierced foam for three-dimensional interest. Test assorted markers on foam scraps to discover how the foam color affects the marker color. Avoid handling a marked area because the ink takes longer to dry on foam than on other surfaces; it is easy to smear or transfer marker colors.

You Will Need

- small food cans, one for each cup; needle-nose pliers
- foam sheets, assorted colors
- scissors with plain or decorative-edge blades
- craft glue
- clothespins, rubber bands
- mat knife and paper punch, optional
- colored markers, optional
- colored tissue paper, shredded paper, or plastic wrap
- assorted treats as desired

1 Compress any rough or sharp edges at upper rim of can, using pliers. Cut 1" (2.5 cm) foam strip with length equal to inner circumference of can. Secure strip to upper inner edge of can, using craft glue; place seam at back. Hold in place with clothespins until dry.

2 Place can on foam sheet; trace around the lower edge. Add design details, such as feathers, feet, or tail beyond traced circle. Cut on outermost lines. Apply glue to inner circle; adhere to bottom of can.

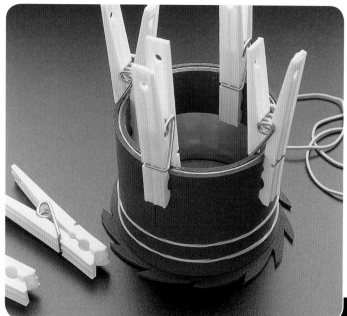

3 Cut foam rectangle with length equal to outer circumference of can and width equal to height of can. Spread craft glue evenly over foam. Secure foam to outer surface of can; place seam at back. Hold in place with clothespins and rubber bands until dry.

4 Draw silhouette pattern, using the examples shown as a guide; add height of can to lower edge of pattern. Cut out pattern and draw around it, using light pencil on dark foam colors; cut out shape.

5 Embellish silhouette as desired; attach foam detail shapes, using glue, for added dimension, or draw design lines, using markers. Cut small slits for inserting dimensional details. Apply glue to extension area of foam only; secure silhouette to back of can, over seam.

6 Add finishing details as desired. Line cup with colored tissue paper, shredded paper, or plastic wrap; fill with treats.

PLACEMATS

Create colorful, sturdy placemats for your guests to enjoy, or let them create their own before sitting down to the party table. Choose from two materials for the placemat. Craft foam sheets, in a rainbow of colors, are the perfect size for rectangular placemats. Liquid spills will bead on the surface until wiped away because these mats are naturally water-resistant. Purchase Kreative Kanvas in oval placemats or large rectangular rugs. One 28" × 36" (71 × 91.5 cm) rug can be cut into four placemats.

Tips for Making Placemats

Design placemat; consider placement of dishes, silver, and napkin. Draw pattern pieces, if desired; trace around base pattern, using pencil.

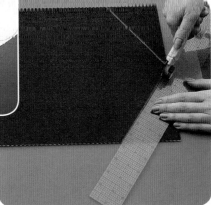

Cut outer edge as desired, using regular or decorative-edge scissors or rotary cutter. Add small shapes, or cut small holes in various shapes and sizes, using paper punches.

Foam placemat with contrasting border. Place two sheets together; mark border. Cut through both layers. Butt border from one sheet to center from second sheet. Glue both pieces to third foam sheet.

You Will Need

- Kreative Kanvas; oval placemats or rectangular rug, cut as above.
- craft foam; 11½" × 17½" (29.3 × 44.3 cm) sheets, in desired colors
- scissors with plain or decorative-edge blades
- mat knife or rotary cutter with plain or decorative blade; cutting surface
- paper punches
- acrylic or latex paints; brushes, for Kreative Kanvas mats
- crayons; paper towel or newsprint; iron, for Kreative Kanvas mats
- sealer; synthetic-bristle paintbrush for Kreative Kanvas mats
- craft glue or low-temperature glue gun, for foam mats
- markers, assorted colors

Color Kreative Kanvas mats, using crayons or paints. Attach shapes, using glue. Outline or add details, using markers. Apply sealer to Kreative Kanvas mats, using paintbrush.

WIRED FELT PLACE CARDS

Bat wings may flap, spiders may crawl, and dragon tails may guard the candy dish when you create these felt place cards for the party table.

Use regular or decorative-edge scissors to cut felt shapes, and bend a small wire sandwiched between felt layers to give them life. Secure a wire extension at the bottom edge of creatures that sit or stand, or push it through the felt for those that fly or crawl.

Use a miniature pumpkin or a small can or box as a base for each place card. Write names directly on the felt creatures or on their bases, using markers.

How to Make a Wired Felt Place Card

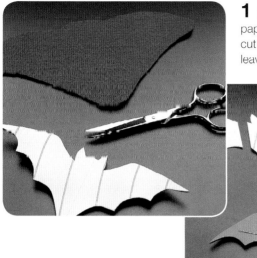

1 Draw design on one side of adhesive sheet; remove paper on other side of the sheet. Adhere design to felt; cut out. Cut second felt piece to the same general shape, leaving ½" (1.3 cm) border all around.

2 Write names on selected pieces, using markers, if desired. Remove remaining paper back and lay felt on table, sticky side up. Cut wire about ⅜" (1 cm) shorter than felt width; lay wire across sticky side of felt.

3 Cut wire the desired length for straight stand. Or, if curl is desired, twist wire around dowel, leaving 1" (2.5 cm) straight at end. Lap short end over shape where desired, or bend short end to 90 degree angle and insert through center of second felt piece.

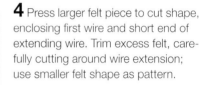

4 Press larger felt piece to cut shape, enclosing first wire and short end of extending wire. Trim excess felt, carefully cutting around wire extension; use smaller felt shape as pattern.

You Will Need

- double-sided adhesive sheet
- felt, assorted colors
- scissors with plain or decorative-edge blades
- paper; chenille stems, optional
- 22- or 24-gauge wire; wire cutter
- ¼" (6 mm) dowel
- miniature pumpkins or small cans
- craft glue
- embellishments as desired

5 Bend wire to shape creature as desired. Insert wire stand into pumpkin base or around stem. Or adhere to candy-filled can covered with felt. Write name on base, if desired.

BUFFET IDEAS

Create a properly ghoulish landscape for your guests, by building a cemetery at the buffet table. Arrange a haunted birdhouse (page 182) at the back of the table; drape the cloth over several hills and let it puddle on the floor. Add a few bare trees near the house. Scatter small monuments across the hills to name the gathered dishes; spatter-paint foam-core or precut wood dome shapes to imitate granite. Set candy worms on caramel apples and cut gelatin shapes with Halloween cookie cutters. Top a pumpkin cake with whipped-cream ghosts and sandwich-cookie tombstones. Slip silverware into napkin ghosts; cinch napkin near the center, enclosing a few cotton balls. Tuck Spanish moss here and there for effect.

Use an interesting collection of baskets to hold all your party fare. Purchase small hay bales at the garden center or craft store; use assorted sizes to raise some baskets above others, if desired. Drape burlap, sprinkle leaves, and nestle gourds and squash of various sizes among the baskets. Create a stuffed sitter (page 180) to rule over the table. Wrap popcorn balls in colorful cellophane, and tie them with wired ribbon. Choose assorted colors of chips, and serve dip in a pumpkin-shaped bowl.

Gather a collection of witches' cauldrons to offer a variety of warm and filling soups, stews, and brews. Arrange one in a tripod centerpiece (page 156). Paint black bowls or mugs with flames licking the sides (page 202). Reveal a favorite spell by placing an open book amid the pots; identify concoctions with hand-lettered notes, and carefully scorch the paper's edges. Select foods with unexpected color, like pistachio pudding. Or use a red decorating gel on marshmallow-topped cookies. Drop dry ice in water dishes hidden behind the cauldrons for an eerie atmosphere; remember to wear gloves when handling dry ice.

PIÑATAS

Wendy Witch flies overhead, filled with candies for your guests. She won't share the treats unless your guests do some tricks, so invite them to break her cache with her own broom.

Use simple papier mâché techniques on a shaped paper bag to form her skirt. Wear rubber gloves and work over a plastic sheet to speed cleanup. Apply a single layer of newspaper strips to provide enough challenge for young goblins; add more layers for stronger, more exuberant guests.

Fill the piñata with small, individually wrapped candies before tying everything together with a strong nylon cord. Purchase a topiary ball at a floral supply store with a green, dense foam head. Choose a low-temperature glue gun to secure details to the head, or the foam may melt. Select assorted black papers to make her dress, cape, hat, and boots; choose colorful papers for her hair and stockings.

Suspend Wendy from a branch, an architectural beam, or a ceiling hook. Catch all the treats on an old sheet or drop cloth for easy collecting of spilled candies when outside.

You Will Need

- paper grocery bag
- stapler
- white craft glue, small bowl, spoon
- newspaper
- plastic sheeting; foam brush, optional
- pie tin; metal washer, 1½" (3.8 cm) wide
- hot glue gun
- screw eye and small dowel
- nylon cord, ⅛" (3 mm)
- topiary ball, 6" (15 cm) diameter; fine sand-paper, optional
- Styrofoam heart, ½" × 3" (1.3 × 7.5 cm); serrated knife, for nose
- small wrapped candies
- acrylic paints
- crepe paper streamer, 1¾" (4.5 cm) wide, black
- scissors with plain or decorative-edge blades
- black tissue paper; ribbon, for cape
- tissue paper, for hair
- black construction paper, three pieces 12½" (31.8 cm) square; light-colored pencil, for hat
- glue-on eyes, 20 mm
- plastic spider
- colored paper in two colors, for legs
- double-sided adhesive sheets, 8½" × 11" (21.8 × 28 cm)
- small broom

How to Make a Piñata

1 Poke ½" (1.3 cm) hole through bottom center of pie tin. Press hole edges flat. Secure washer over hole, covering compressed edges, using hot glue.

2 Sand foam ball lightly with fine sandpaper to remove ridges, if necessary; wipe with damp rag. Insert screw eye in end of dowel. Cut 3 yd. (2.75 m) length of cord; slip end through screw eye and knot ends together. Tie second knot over first; tighten knots. Insert dowel through washer, tin, and ball center. Push ball tightly against pie tin; knot cord just above ball. Remove screw eye from dowel.

(Continued)

3 Cut heart in half, using serrated knife. Compress hard edges of outer curve, shaping as desired. Curve cut edge slightly to fit contour of ball. Glue to ball at desired nose location.

4 Crumple paper bag to soften hard edges. Push four corners in, rounding bottom; staple corner layers together on inside. Stack newspaper layers; tear 1½" (3.8 cm) strips, using straight edge, if desired. Blend ¼ cup (50 ml) glue with ¼ cup (50 ml) water in small bowl.

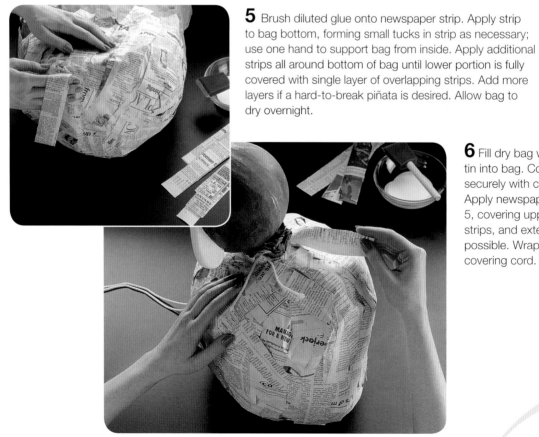

5 Brush diluted glue onto newspaper strip. Apply strip to bag bottom, forming small tucks in strip as necessary; use one hand to support bag from inside. Apply additional strips all around bottom of bag until lower portion is fully covered with single layer of overlapping strips. Add more layers if a hard-to-break piñata is desired. Allow bag to dry overnight.

6 Fill dry bag with treats. Tuck pie tin into bag. Compress bag top; tie securely with cord, forming neck. Apply newspaper strips as in step 5, covering upper bag; lap lower strips, and extend strips as high as possible. Wrap strip around neck, covering cord. Dry thoroughly.

7 Paint bag black; paint head and nose as desired. Allow to dry. Attach wiggly eyes, using hot glue. Paint mouth as desired.

8 Stretch one edge of streamer gently to ruffle edge. Attach the straight edge to piñata body, using undiluted glue. Start at center bottom, spiraling upward; lap each layer over previous layer about 1" (2.5 cm).

9 Fuse two layers of colored paper, using double-sided adhesive sheet. Cut four strips 2" (5 cm) wide. Accordion-fold each strip; glue and lap ends to join two strips for each leg.

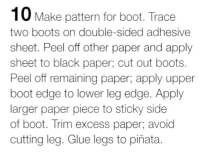

10 Make pattern for boot. Trace two boots on double-sided adhesive sheet. Peel off other paper and apply sheet to black paper; cut out boots. Peel off remaining paper; apply upper boot edge to lower leg edge. Apply larger paper piece to sticky side of boot. Trim excess paper; avoid cutting leg. Glue legs to piñata.

(Continued)

11 Fold tissue paper in half; mark two arcs 1¼" and 14" (3.2 and 35.5 cm) from fold corner. Cut on both lines through all layers, for cape; open. Tie cape around neck, using ribbon.

12 Cut tissue strips for hair ¾" (2 cm) wide, using decorative-edge scissors, if desired. Attach hair to head, using glue; layer long strips on back and sides to cover lower three-quarters of head. Position short strips for bangs.

13 Mark center of first hat square, using colored pencil. Measure and draw two circles around center mark; the smaller radius is 2½" (6.5 cm), the larger is 5" (12.5 cm). Cut out both circles for brim. Cut another brim, using first as pattern.

14 Measure 11½" and 12½" (29.3 and 31.8 cm) arcs from corner of third square; cut on outer arc for hat crown. Cut from crown edge to inner arc at ½" (1.3 cm) intervals. Bend paper along inner arc for tabs.

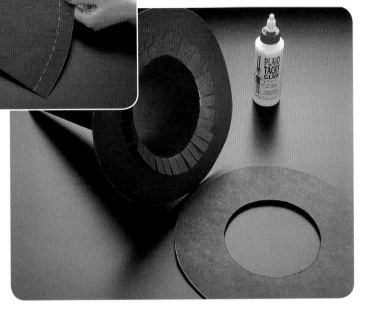

15 Lap straight edges of crown about 2¼" (6 cm); drop one brim over peak. Glue tabs to underside of brim, using undiluted craft glue. Glue second brim to first brim, aligning edges and enclosing tabs. Slip hat over cord until it rests on head. Glue hat overlap. Attach plastic spider on hat, using hot glue. Suspend piñata as desired.

More Ideas for Piñatas

Make a dragon piñata. Quarter a Styrofoam ball for the mouth and add small pom-poms for nostrils. Make horns, spikes, and teeth from colored paper.

Peter Pumpkin doesn't need a head; just a friendly smile. Cap him off with a papier mâché stem, paper leaves, and wire-core paper twist tendrils.

MUMMY HANDS

Every mummy would love to be the life of the party! Grant that wish by letting the mummy lend you a hand or two at your next ghostly celebration.

Imitate a mummy's bandaged hand by wrapping a surgical glove, available at drugstores, with torn strips of aged batiste. Add a jeweled ring, if desired, to indicate a lifetime of wealth.

Consider a useful task that the hand may do, and shape the fingers in a way that seems to bring the mummy to life. Set the hand amid a candlescape and place a match between two fingers. Set a hand beneath a lamp's pull chain. Or gently shape two hands around a cauldron for the buffet table.

How to Make a Mummy Hand

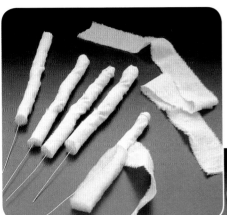

1 Tea-dye batiste; allow to dry. Tear into 1½" (3.8 cm) strips. Cut five 10" (25.5 cm) lengths of wire and five 1" × 7" (2.5 × 18 cm) strips of batting. Wrap a batting strip around each wire; secure with fabric strips and glue.

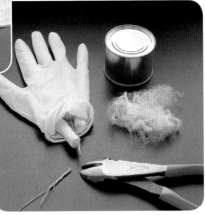

2 Insert one wrapped wire into each finger of glove; twist ends together, and trim. Insert small amount of batting to fill out palm area, if necessary. Stretch glove around can for support; tape in place.

3 Dip batiste strip into fabric stiffener. Wrap end over fingertip; turn strip, and wrap down finger. Press excess onto palm or back of hand. Continue wrapping all fingers. Wrap hand, covering entire glove and can completely. Wrap fingers and hand with several layers, for more support. Shape hand as desired; allow to dry.

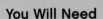

You Will Need

- batiste, tea
- tape, 20-gauge wire, wire cutter
- polyester batting
- craft glue
- latex glove
- small unopened food can
- fabric stiffener
- match; orange felt scrap, optional
- glue gun and glue sticks

4 Wrap dry hand with layer of dry batiste strips, securing with hot glue as necessary. Leave occasional loose tail. Add any details, such as wooden match.

Patterns

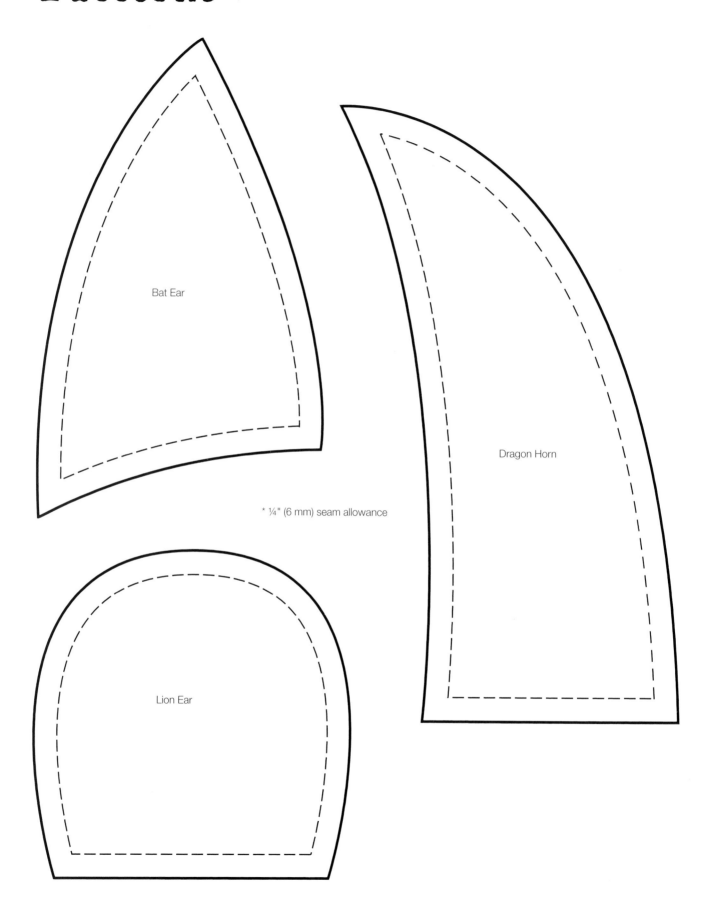

Bat Ear

* ¼" (6 mm) seam allowance

Dragon Horn

Lion Ear

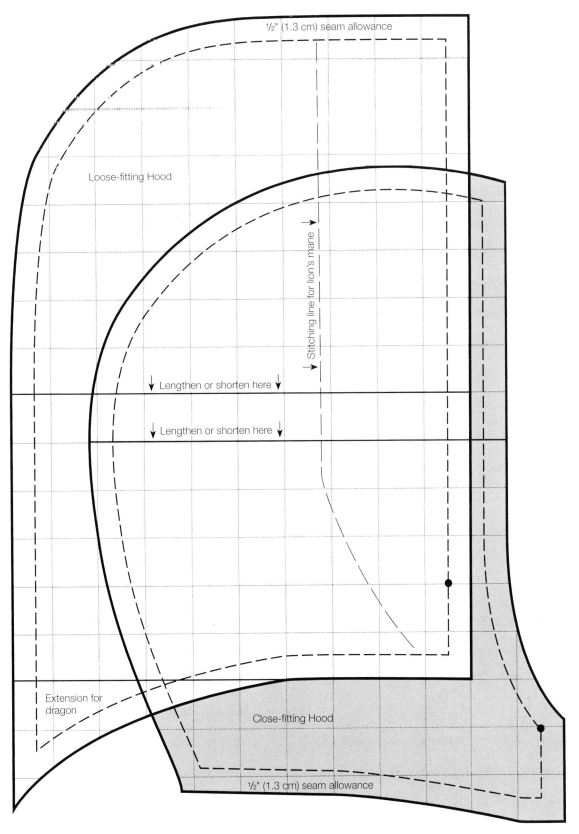

½" (1.3 cm) seam allowance

Loose-fitting Hood

Stitching line for lion's mane

↓ Lengthen or shorten here ↓

↓ Lengthen or shorten here ↓

Extension for dragon

Close-fitting Hood

½" (1.3 cm) seam allowance

1 square = 1" (2.5 cm)

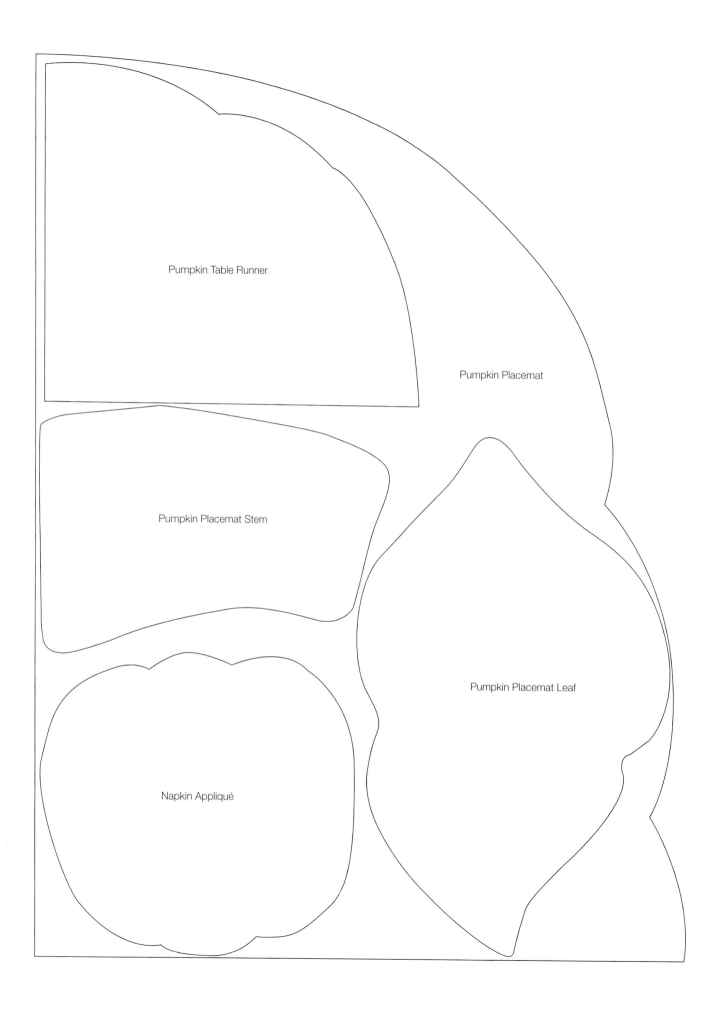

Pumpkin Table Runner

Pumpkin Placemat

Pumpkin Placemat Stem

Pumpkin Placemat Leaf

Napkin Appliqué

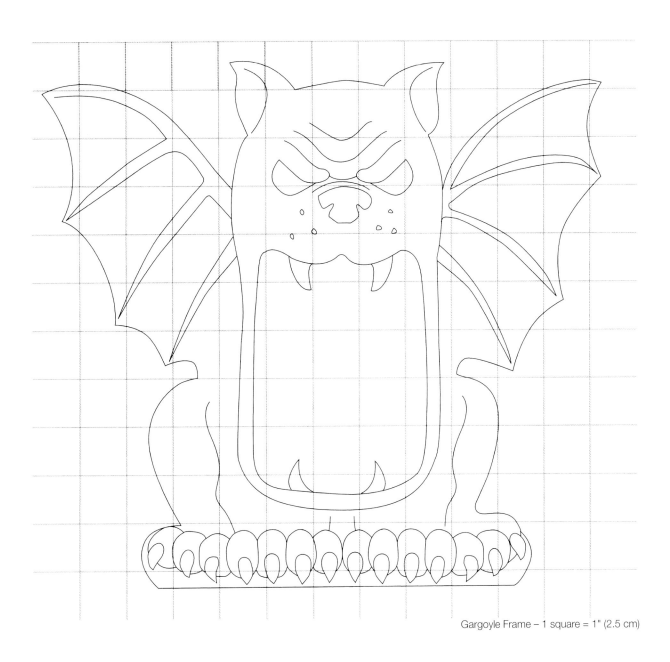

Gargoyle Frame – 1 square = 1" (2.5 cm)

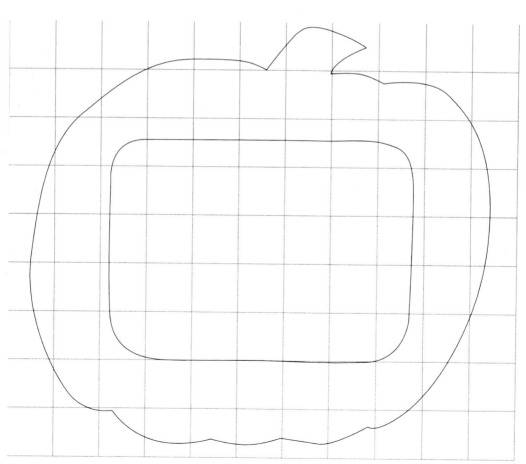

Pumpkin Frame – 1 square = 1" (2.5 cm)

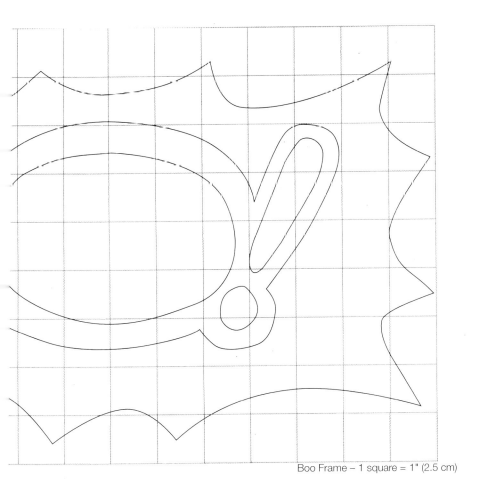

Boo Frame – 1 square = 1" (2.5 cm)

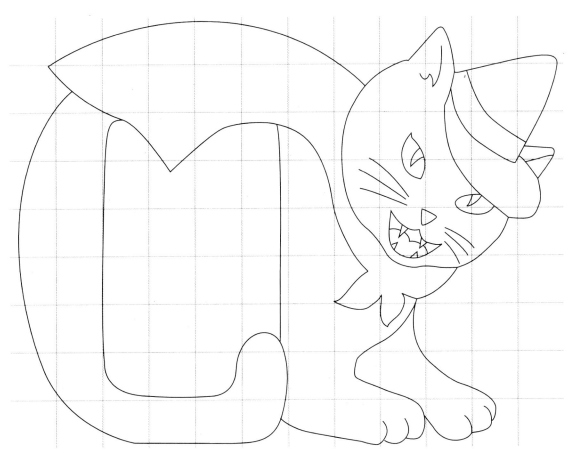

Kitty Frame – 1 square = 1" (2.5 cm)

Pumpkin Carving Patterns (enlarge to desired size)

Table Runner Cat

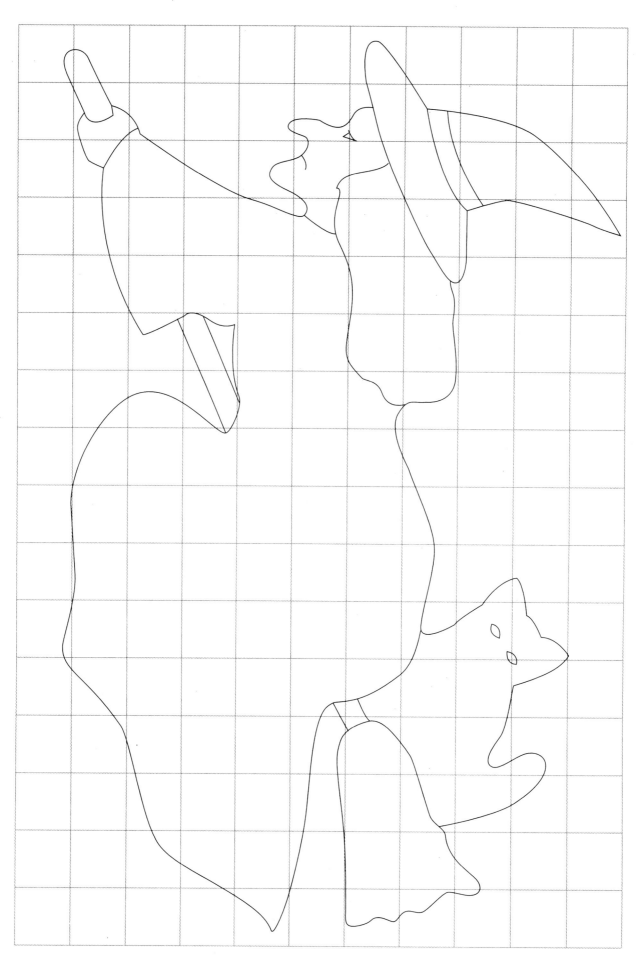

Welcome Witch – 1 square = 1" (2.5 cm)

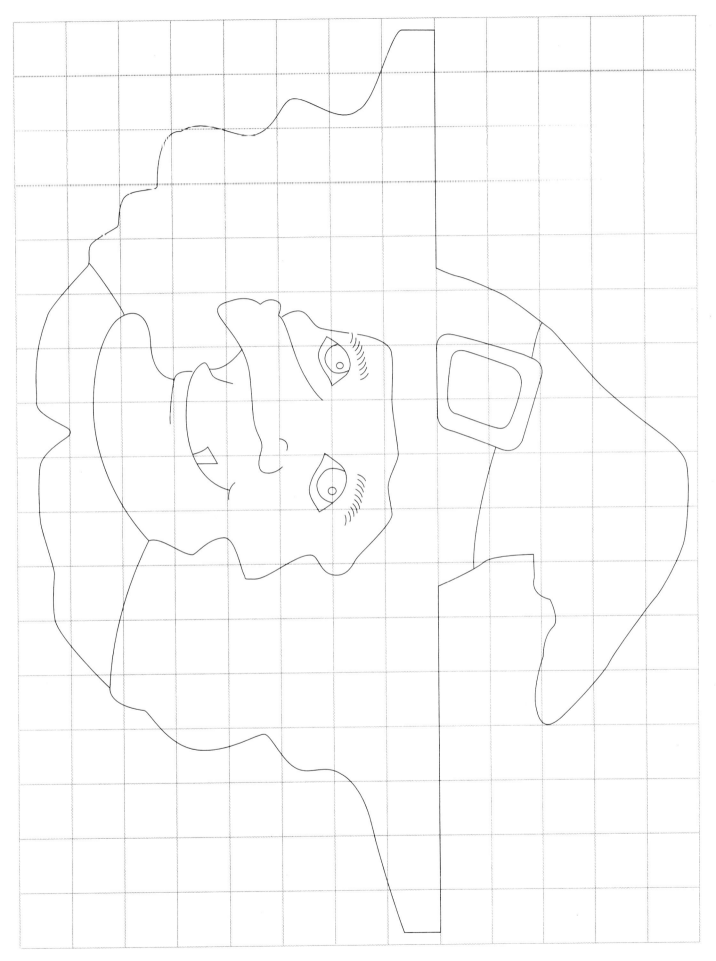

Witch Shelf – 1 square = 1" (2.5 cm)

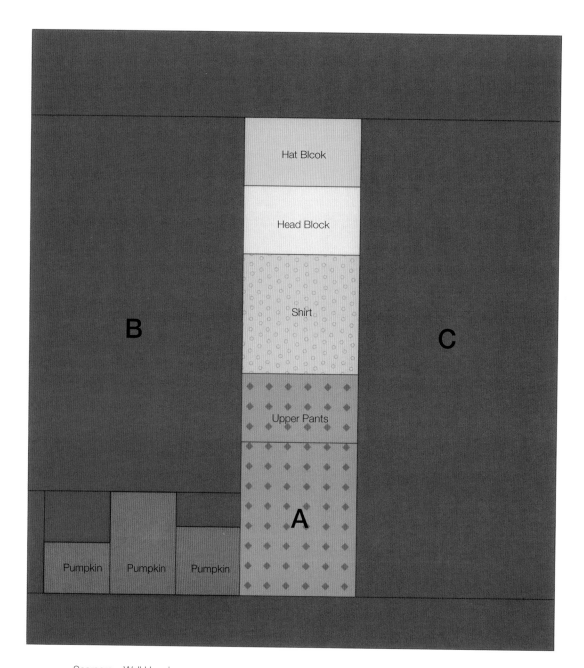

Scarecrow Wall Hanging

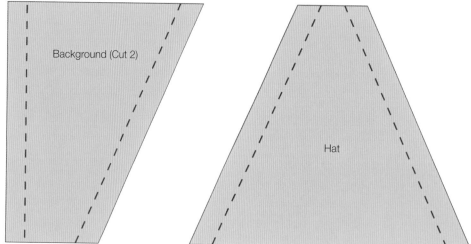

Index

A

angel costume, 11

animal paw glove, 108–109

anklets, 102–105

antennae, 60, 66–67

appliqués, 28–29

armbands, 102–107

B

ball cap headpiece, 60, 62

bat costume, 13, 82–87

    ear pattern, 228

bee costumes, 12

birdhouse decorations, 182–185

black-tie skeleton

    decoration, 162–165

buffet decorating ideas, 218–219

butterfly costume, 12

C

capes, 70–75

claws, 108–109, 111

coasters, 196–197, 201

collars, 98–99

    for capes, 74

    flat, 99–100

    gathered, 98–99, 101

costumes, in general, 8–9

    examples of, 10–13

    foundation garments for, 10

    safety and comfort in, 14–15

crowns and halos, 50–53

cups, for party treats, 210–213

D

design blocked tabards, 20–21

design inserts, 37

dragon costume, 13, 20

    spiked hood for, 54–56, 58, 228, 229

E

ears, 60, 63, 228

elastic harness, for wings, 91

elastic-waist skirt, 76–78

eyes, 65

F

fabric collage, 208

fairy princess costume, 11

felt bat wings, 87

felt cape, 74–75

felt place cards, 216–217

flat collars, 99–100

foam treat cups, 210–213

foundation garments, 10

Frankenstein shelf sitter, 186–188

full suit costumes, 36–39

G

gathered sleeves, for gowns, 35

gathered wristlets and

    anklets, 102–105

ghostly outdoor trick-or-

    treater decoration, 130–133

glass serving pieces, 202–205

gloves, 108–111

gowns, 30–35

gypsy costume, 13

H

Halloween swag, 152–155

halos, 50–53

harlequin table runner, 192–195

harvest wreath decorations, 148–151

hats and headwear, 40–67

haunted birdhouses, 182–185

headbands, covering, 60–61

headwear, 40–67

hoods, padded, 54–59, 229

horns, 64

house decorations

    indoor, 146–189

    outdoor, 122–145

    party, 190–227

I

indoor decorations, 146–189

invitations, 206–209

J

jack-o'-lantern costume, 11

L

leaf skirt, 80–81

leggings, 102–103, 107

legs, tails, and stingers, 22–27

lighted swag, 142–143

lined cape, 70–73

lion costume, 11, 36

    lion's mane hood, 54–57

M

magician costume, 11

magician's wand, 116–119

medieval hats, 46–49

mobile decoration, 166–171

mummy hand decoration, 226–227

N

nails, for gloves, 108–109, 111

napkins, 196–197, 200, 230

O

outdoor decorations, 122–145

overlay, for skirt, 79

P

padded armbands, 102–103, 105–106

padded hoods, 54–59

padded wings, 88–91

painted glass serving pieces, 202–205

party decorations, 190–227

paw glove, 108–109

petal hood, 54–56, 59

petal skirt, 80–81

pet, costume for, 12

picture frames, 178–181, 231–233

piñatas, 220–225

place cards, 216–217

placemats, 196–199, 214–215, 230

pumpkin costume, 11, 16

pumpkins, carving and
    painting, 124–129, 234

pumpkin table linens, 196–201, 230

R

robot costume, 13

royal couple costumes, 13

royal scepter, 116–117, 119

rugs, stenciled, 144–145

S

safety and comfort, 14–15

scarecrow outdoor
    decoration, 138–141

scarecrow wall hanging, 172–177

scepters, 116–119

shelf decorations
    witch, 160–161, 237
        wooden sitters for, 186–189

shoe flaps, 38–39

skeleton decoration, 162–165

skirts, 76–81

spats, 112–115

spiderweb mobile, 166–171

stamps, cutting and using, 209

star wand, 116–118

stenciled rugs, 144–145

stingers, 22–27

superhero costume, 11

swags
    Halloween, 152–155
    lighted, 142–143

T

tabards, 16–21

table centerpiece, 156–159

table decoration ideas, 218–219

table linens, 196–201,
    214–215, 230, 235

table runners, 192–195, 199, 230, 235

tails, 22–27

tin man costume, 14

treat bag invitations, 206–209

treat cups, 210–213

trick-or-treater dummy, 130–133

tripod centerpiece, 156–159

V

vent hoses, for armbands and
    leggings, 102–103, 107

W

wall hanging, 172–177

wands, 116–119

wings
    bat, 82–87
    padded, 88–91
    sheer, 92–95

wired felt place cards, 216–217

witch costume, 10
    hats for, 42–45

witch decorations
    indoor shelf, 160–161, 237
    outdoor, 134–137, 236

wizard costume, 12

wand for, 116–119

wooden shelf sitters, 186–189

wreaths, 148–151

wristlets, 102–105

Z

zinnia costume, 10